LIFE IS A PACK OF 52 CARDS

LIFE IS A PACK OF 52 CARDS

SUMEET JAIN

GOOD TIMES

GOOD TIMES BOOKS PVT. LTD.
New Delhi (India)
www.goodtimesbooks.com

Published by

GOOD TIMES BOOKS PVT. LTD.

H-13, Bali Nagar, New Delhi-110 015 (INDIA)
Phones: +91-11-25913301, 45069086 Fax: +91-11-45069086
Email : info@goodtimesbooks.com
Website : www.goodtimesbooks.com

First Good Times Edition 2013
ISBN-13 : 978-93-806196-7-5

Cataloging in Publication Data--DK
Courtesy: D.K. Agencies (P) Ltd. <docinfo@dkagencies.com>

Jain, Sumeet.
Life is a pack of 52 cards / Sumeet Jain. -- 1st Good Times ed.
p. cm.
ISBN 9789380619675

1. Life skills. I. Title.

DDC 646.7 23

Printed in India at
Salasar Imaging Systems

The author is grateful to have spent some wonderful time with LIFE in its various moods, which have taught him the immaculate "Life lessons": how to be truthful, affirmative, compassionate, realistic and humble, even during the most difficult situations that one might have to face.

This book is a tribute to the greatest teacher of all times—LIFE.

Acknowledgements

I dedicate my first ever writing experience to the sun (my junior) and shine (my soul mate) of my life—for their true love, deep faith and endless patience. They gave me all the time I needed, in solitude, to think and write—even if that meant dealing with some of the issues on their own, without involving me. Without their support, this book would have never reached your hands and landed in your book-shelf.

I am a strong believer of inheritance(s)—through genes. Therefore, I am very thankful to have picked up virtues, like attention to detail, contentment and patience, from my father. To my mother I am thankful for her: self-confidence, deftness and extrovert nature; the very attributes that I have genetically inherited from her.

I also take this as an opportunity to thank a few cherished friends who helped me with the initial review of this book. Alongside, let me also thank my official reviewer for being patient and thorough. He improved my manuscript immeasurably. He read and reread every word, and has instilled a freshness in the book which gives it a more contemporary feel.

A team is as good as its captain. In my case, the team is me and my book merged as one, and the captain is my publisher—who believed in me and gave me a chance to share my experiences with the external world. It is indeed a dream come true for someone who had been reading their books for years, to now author one, published by them.

I would also like to thank my editor. Over a period of time she became a good friend of mine, and continues to be my guide and mentor in the world of publishing.

Contents

♣

Acknowledgements 7
Prologue 11

1. Only a Cat has Nine Lives! 15
2. Be Brutal 18
3. Dial 'Yes' for Disaster 22
4. Gold Standard 27
5. Don't be a Dinosaur 31
6. Great Expectations 35
7. Living Life, One Day At A Time 39
8. It is All about the Franchise and the Character 43
9. Max Payne vs. Call of Duty 46
10. Did you Get Hurt? 49
11. Have You Trained Your Commanders Well? 51
12. Have We Forgotten "Him"? 55
13. Eat that Frog! 58
14. You are Not Immortal! 60
15. Rise Like a Phoenix! 63
16. Always Outnumbered, but Never Outmanned 68
17. Pride and Prejudice 71
18. The 13-letter Word 73

19. Follow the Dollar 78
20. Don't be a Bozo 80
21. Secret of the Dragon Scroll 83
22. Instant Redemption 86
23. Getting on Your Soapbox? Watch Out! 89
24. Choose Your Own Race! 92
25. Being Human! 96
26. Nothing Stays Forever! 100
27. Don't be a Black Hole 103
28. Do Yourself a Favor...Meet Them 107
29. Everyone Counts 112
30. Learning from the Game 116
31. The 'HQ' Test 123
32. There are a Few Things that Money Can't Buy 127
33. Mentoring Matters 131
34. Have you Tasted a Blowfish Yet? 134
35. Royal Empires 138
36. Live for Greatness 141
37. Die for Greatness 145
38. The Gift from God! 148
39. Have Guts...Bell the Cat! 153
40. The Law of Opposites 157
41. The KYF Mantra 163
42. Finish your Meal 170
43. You are the Boss 175
44. Do you Treat them Royally? 179
45. Last Mile Connectivity 186
46. Let us Un-complicate 192
47. Everyone is in Sales 198
48. Over-speeding Thrills, but Kills 204
49. Wanna Shine? Polish! 208
50. The Hunter and the Cook Story 212
51. The '007' Principles 217
52. Say Cheese! 228

Epilogue 233

Prologue

How it all happened?
Well…it simply happened!

Out on a vacation, as we were relaxing, my wife gave me the idea to write a book—or at least try my hand at writing one. Having known me for many years now, my love for books too is not unknown to her. Furthermore, being a witness to how my son and I had been filling racks with books, year after year, she thought it was time that I tried my hand at writing one. The one liner from her, which sounded like a 'mission statement'... "Write on something that your son can be proud of, when *he* grows up"...served as the clarion call. I finally said, "Yes" to writing this book—if not for myself, at least for my son and wife.

Armed with the ignorance of a novice and inspiration of an artist as I set out on this journey, the first question that gripped me was its theme. I have always believed in life being the greatest teacher of all. Furthermore, *life*—God's wondrous gift—is *that beautiful process* which differentiates us from millions of planets and stars. Hence, I chose to write on my personal experiences: how they affected me and thus, taught me the precious lessons in life, which I reverently refer to as my "Life lessons."

One question inevitably leads to another. So, the next one was the title: what to call my maiden writing venture...and my *take* on life led me to the title. I have always treated life like a pack of 52 cards, to win the games that we are required to play every day. At times, you (will) find that you have an ace up your sleeves, while sometimes you just get a '2' or a '3'—and at other times it is (either) a 'joker' (or) and a 'trump card' that make(s) you happy. Further to this, there are times, when even a sequence of '2' can lead you to win a game, while even with the 'King' or the 'Queen' on your side you could lose everything. Last but not the least, remember those occasions when you just played it 'blind?' Well, that is how life is—very unpredictable, yet a very powerful teacher, for all of us. Thus, the decision to name my book as a simile to a pack of cards. Each card describes a moment of my life gift-wrapped as a chapter (the book has 52 carefully chosen chapters from my life), with the prologue and epilogue as two 'joker' cards, which come along with a standard pack of cards!

Okay! I now had a theme, title and storyline for my book. But how would I get the time to write it, was the next question that needed to be answered. My style of work always involves: setting a goal first, which is then divided into milestones; then a 'target date' is fixed to achieve each milestone; and finally I go all out to complete it—on time. The same approach I followed for this book as well. Since I had decided upon 52 chapters, so I set up a year's (52 weeks) timeline to complete the same. Thus, a commitment was made. And once I make a commitment I don't even listen to myself!

Life has always been a game of choices for me. It is a play of perceptions, from which we draw conclusions—and project the associated outlook every day. To some, life appears always as 'half-full,' while for others it is 'half-empty.' In one of the world's most loved movie series, *Spiderman*, the protagonist ponders at the end of the climax when all the conflicts, hardships and confusions have cleared away...and gives voice to one of life's best lessons:

"No matter what the circumstances are, we always have a choice. And, the choices that we make in life determine who we are?"

How true! The choices that we make in our life, indeed determine the kind of results that we experience and the quality of the life that we live.

I am reminded of Robin Sharma, writing in one of his books:

"Everyone who enters your life, has a lesson to teach and a story to tell. Every person you pass, during the moments that make up your days, represents an opportunity to show a little more of the compassion and courtesy that defines your humanity." Well said, Robin! You have been one of my sources of inspiration, to choose 'life' as the theme of my first book.

You will meet a lot of people in this book. Some may remind you of yourself, while others may just seem familiar. As I share these personal experiences (I have changed names to honor and respect the privacy of the persons concerned), possibilities of your having had such experiences already, are quite high. And since we all are unique, you must have dealt with such situations in unique ways, different from mine. I look forward to hear from all of you about your personal experiences, on my book's Facebook page or on the website of this book: *www.lifeisapackof52cards.com*.

For the 'read-aholics,' this book is very 'small and thin,' since the chapters are concise and short. Each chapter is easy to read, with a message at the end. I strongly believe in the power of quotes as they contain a plethora of values, even though they are confined to one or two lines. Hence, I have tried my level best to end each chapter with a quote by the famous people whom I have read over the years and felt—and feel—blessed by the same.

1 Only a Cat has Nine Lives!

♣

Unlike cats, we just have one life to live and make the most of. Life is one of the greatest gifts that God has blessed us with. As Robert Byrne quotes, "The purpose of life, is a life of purpose." Life is like a savings bank account. How you spend it, is entirely your call. This bank account too has some unique features. So that it does not become dormant, you need to operate it from time to time. And there are a few simple ways to make deposits to it and increase your life's bank balance: smile, be good to others, take care of your body, eat well, help the needy, enjoy your relationships, invest in friendship, live for a cause and live with a purpose. With these deposits, see how you get happiness in return, that too at a very high interest rate. A quote by Ralph Waldo Emerson: "It is not the length of life, but the depth of life which matters," comes to my mind. When you deeply ponder on it you will be able to realize how brilliant an observation it is.

You need to celebrate life every day—to the fullest—and not only on the special occasions. By doing so life in totality becomes more enjoyable. Moreover, I have come across many people who, after a certain period of time, chose not to celebrate their anniversaries, birthdays and other special days. When I asked the reason, few said they were too old to celebrate their birthdays; while some were always out on official trips, with no time to celebrate even the special moments. And a few of them didn't even care about them anymore. They were all running blindly—

almost breathlessly—chasing wealth, fame and success. But, somewhere down the line, they have failed to realize that their life's bank balance has been shrinking all these years and very soon, they would have to file for bankruptcy. After all, as John Ruskin says, "There is no wealth, but life." The sooner we realize this, the better.

I remember one of my friends, who used to celebrate each and every occasion he felt was important in his life. Not that he looked for reasons to hit the bar. (For that, God made Fridays! Thank you, God!) His theory was simple and plain: "Most of the times, we limit our celebrations in anticipation of achieving something incredible and 'big.' We search for reasons to celebrate and in doing so, we forget the beautiful occasions that life sends our way, every other day. There was a time when I celebrated each notable difference in my daughter as she grew up. It was a bliss watching her grow. Till a certain period, my daughter never felt the need for celebrating her birthdays. Now, when I meet many of my friends they envy me, even though they are thousand times richer than me. They envy the art of celebrating happiness that I have mastered over the years. And believe it or not, it reflects on your face. That is how they 'see' it. It is very important to aim high, set goals, achieve success, earn money and fame...and all that. I am not against them at all. After all, money makes your life easier and comfortable. It is like walking on the road, and someone offers you a ride so that you reach your destination faster. But, what if the car has black glasses through which you can't see what is happening outside? That is where I have an issue. Most of the people today are on the fast lane to success—and drive a car which has black glasses. I acknowledge the fact that their cars will make them reach the destination faster than you can imagine. Yet, at the same time, they are missing out on all the fun. The roadside motels, the sceneries, the people you meet...and the like...according to me, is so much fun. While their 'green' bank balance continues to swell, their life's bank balance continues to plummet."

What my friend said is not difficult to achieve. All you need to do is start making small deposits in your life's bank account.

Pick up the phone and chat with your old friends; make frequent visits to your parents/in-laws; go to old-age homes, schools for the blind, orphanages and spend time with the inmates there; take your spouse out for a surprise candlelight dinner; give a surprise visit to your children's school and pick them up; have a session of video games or a game of football with your kids; greet your colleagues on their success, promotions, birthdays...*celebrate with all and life will celebrate you*. Such small investments—those deposits—will yield compound interest at a rate unimagined ever, and will make you richer immeasurably with each passing day.

Yet, all these years, we thought getting rich was the toughest goal to achieve! ☺.

Now that I have hopefully given you a formula to get rich, let me end this chapter with a great quote by **Helen Keller**, American author and educator:

"Many persons have a wrong idea of what constitutes true happiness. It is not attained through self-gratification, but through fidelity to a worthy purpose."

2 Be Brutal

Each year, around the same time I take a week-long sabbatical from my professional life and go for an out-of-town vacation. Since I have been following this routinely for years, it has now become more of a habit for me. With conviction in the power of planning well ahead of time, so that I can be ready for what the future has in store, my mantra for planning has been: *failing to plan is planning to fail*. As Zig Ziglar writes in one of his books, "Winners evaluate themselves in a positive manner and look for their strengths, as they work to overcome their weaknesses."

I have always used this quote as a means to self-evaluate—critically—and rate myself with respect to various parameters, which I laid out as essential as per my own definition of success. Thus, I always find time to prepare an annual report of my own self so that I can use it for two things: to assess how I fared against the benchmarks I had set the previous year; and to envisage how to use these to set benchmarks for the coming year.

In the context I remember the guidance of one of my bosses. He observed:

> "This is one of the most contentious subjects for the younger generation. Most of the companies are through with their appraisal by March end each year. It is when you feel the heat in the air. Do you know why? Because, youngsters these days have forgotten the art of self-

evaluation. They seem to be living in a hypothetical world, where they crown themselves the undisputed kings. And you know what will happen when you tell a king that he is not doing his job properly! Swords will be drawn. In fact, some of my best performers who have fine-tuned themselves through self-evaluation, haven't met me for years. They simply know that they don't need an appraisal as they are aware of their strengths and weaknesses very clearly. They don't want a person like me to tell them about the same. They do a 'SWOT' (it is a term used in management, and stands for strengths, weaknesses, opportunities and threats) analysis on themselves and know exactly where they stand, and what should be their next step.

The off-shoot of this good habit reflects in their work. They are good at what they do. Their work does not require much touch-up, because they are their biggest critics. They review their work so thoroughly that I rarely feel compelled to attach a quality analyst with them. I remember a girl who once worked for me. She was simply *the best*. She was very particular about her work, and devoted a good deal of time going through it over and over again. There were times, when I tried to convince her to submit whatever she had already completed. But, she wouldn't budge. She would work extra hours to ensure all that she delivered was just awesome. And hence, I always forwarded the assignments completed by her without even having a glance at it. The question of 'checking' it never arose, because I believed that a 'work packet' sealed with her approval would not need the perusal by a second pair of eyes. Unfortunately, such dedicated people have become very rare nowadays.

But all can emulate her. For that, you have to treat your career like your own professional brand. And as a good marketing strategist, it is important to see if your brand is going in the right direction or not. It is important to carefully position its USPs and focus on areas which will set you apart from the maddening crowd. I have been an avid follower of Jack Trout and have always believed: to win the battles raging in the mind of the prospective clients—to win them over—it is important to find that 'uniqueness' first which will differentiate you from others, and then maintain the 'focus' on it. I have never believed in 'line extensions,' and have always felt that while it may help you achieve some short-term gains, it will ultimately erode your main brand value over the years. Hence, it is imperative for the present generation to sustain the focus on their unique strengths, and to critically evaluate them every year. By doing so, they thus would keep it alive and kicking, even in the midst of toughest of competitions that time has to offer.

Talking about our goals, it is essential that we concentrate more on setting the 'right' goals for ourselves. And while we set our goals we must also keep in mind: *impossible is possible.* As Frank Typer defines it brilliantly:

> *'Goals must be beyond your grasp but within your reach. While we critically review these goals, if we find that they have not succeeded in keeping our USPs intact, then it is high time to take a very detailed stock—of our very own selves and make corrections before it is too late. I assure you, if we can get into the habit of self-evaluation we will never need an external appraisal to tell us who we are, what went wrong and what was accomplished well. After all, you cannot escape from yourself—as you cannot deceive your conscience.'"*

Till date, I have never forgotten his advice and have followed it as much as possible. In this context, here is another honest confession about a habit of mine. This being my first writing venture, when I was halfway into this book only then did I realize that my writing style had improved a lot. I *knew* what to write and how to write. So after the completion of the first draft, the first person to review it was none other than myself. As the review was underway, I had to acknowledge that the first few chapters were not as impressive as the ones which were written later—the ones which form the latter half of the book. It also dawned on me that just the way I lose interest in a book, if the first few pages are not impressive, my readers too would lose interest to continue with it. Therefore, after completing the review, I took many more weeks and put in more effort to make all the chapters equally attractive—and satisfying—to the author as well as the reader in me.

Self-evaluation is an indispensable tool if you wish to succeed in life. This truth my boss used to convey through his words:

"Evaluate yourself brutally and show no mercy. If you show mercy, the world will be a lot crueler."

3 Dial 'Yes' for Disaster

Corporate houses spend millions of dollars, *every year*, to send their key personnel of the management to attend workshops on effective time-management. Well, I do not rebuff the importance of such trainings. But at the same time, I can definitely suggest one great method to effectively manage your time—without spending the huge amount of money that is spent for such workshops *every year*!

Somehow, we have gotten into this 'bad' habit of saying 'yes' to everything that comes our way. Robin Sharma terms this habit of saying 'yes' to everything: "Bankruptcy by yes." And I too find it to be so true!

On a typical 'working day,' you will be constantly bombarded by people who try to hijack your time by bringing in their own priorities. This, they then try to push hard, to take top slots on your priority list. Come to think of it, most of the time we too end up doing the same!

Picture this: you get a phone call. As you pick up the phone the person at the other end has a very urgent task for you. You hang up, promising to do it by the end of your day—and hence, add it to your already fully loaded 'to do' list for the day. The very next thing that you see, is a new e-mail indicator on your computer's taskbar. You open it, only to find that a new report has being asked for submission—that too urgently. You are left with no choice but to add this too, to your list.

And from experience, such incidents are commonplace at our workplace!

It is very true that learning to say 'no' to each and every task that comes your way, is one of the most difficult things to do. Reasons could be many. When you say 'no' to someone, you may be instantly branded: rude, non-cooperative and insensitive. The ego might even lead some to take this 'no' as an act of defiance. And I encounter this trend more in my country than anywhere else. I always tell my staff to learn to say 'no'—from the West. They are so good at managing their time well only because they really do not care about upsetting anyone who just pops out from nowhere. *But back here, it is easier said than done.*

I am reminded of one such incident. It was when my BlackBerry e-mails suddenly stopped working one day. I was traveling, and had no other means to keep in touch. So, I frantically made calls to our help desk in United States to bail me out of this situation. The person on the other side listened to my problem with care. When I was through with my 'reporting,' I asked, "So, can I expect this to be sorted out in the next few minutes?" His reply was: "It seems to be a very small issue and will not take me more than 5 minutes. However, my list for the day is full. So, the best that I can do is take it up tomorrow morning and fix it." Just as everyone else does, I too insisted, "If it is just going to take 5 minutes, can't you simply fix it now, since it is impacting my business very badly." He was polite, yet firm, and gave me an ETA (expected time to accomplish) of the next business day. At that instant I was frustrated. But later on, I appreciated the guy for his time-management skills. I even wrote to him, appreciating his habit: sticking with what was on his plate and completing it first. Vis-à-vis, when I picture the same incident in my country, I envision the guy on the phone saying, "Sure sir. We will get this done in a few minutes." But in most of the cases, those 'few minutes' would not be before the next business day.

Thus, one of the areas where my clients frequently raise concern is the habit of their Indian team: the team says "Yes" to everything, even though they keep telling the team to frankly say "No" if some tasks seem difficult. But their pleas fall to deaf ears.

As with everything, this habit too has its flip side, with many woes attached:

- You lose trust. Once you are not able to deliver something on time, as promised, people start taking you as a latecomer—having least regard for time.
- You have the same 'work hours' every day like others. So, if you complete the one which was not originally on the list, chances are, you will do it at the expense of the one which was originally on that list. And with it, you render others dissatisfied. In reality, the "Yes" that you said in trying to momentarily please somebody, will have a more devastating effect as compared to having said an honest, "No," along with mentioning a reasonable timeline required to accomplish the assignment.

It is therefore always advisable to not get carried away by the 'urgent' matters that 'others' bring to the table for you every day. Be polite, yet firm. Be honest in your responses. By being honest about taking up—and not taking up—new tasks, you not only make your life easy and relaxed, you also develop a great character—a character that people would love to get associated with.

There was once a manager—hard-working and very diligent—who worked for me. But he was afflicted with this bad habit of never saying a 'no'—not even to me, though I was aware of his workload. On a number of occasions I explained to him that it is absolutely okay to say a 'no,' if he had his plate full; but he never listened. Fortunately, I met his family (in his absence) one day at a shopping mall. After greeting them I asked for him, and it was then something was revealed to me: his wife shared that he had been busy trying to complete some urgent work that was entrusted to him (by me). At that very moment, I felt like a criminal, standing in front of his family. I had never realized that this guy accepted everything I poured on him—and because of this, his family suffered immensely as they lost out on spending quality time together.

Being always available is another variant of this habit...and I mean it literally. That is what I figured out after meeting a few such people in my life. There is one such person I cannot forget ever. He would always take calls, and respond to chats—even if that meant responding at the middle of the night. God! I don't know how his family felt, but I surely felt terrible. I saw him hurting himself in two ways: it took a heavy toll on his health and he set a wrong precedence for his peers—not to mention the perception he created, of 'being available all the time,' which made people take him lightly. They never had any respect for his time, always assuming: no matter what, he would do it.

In fact, we have extended this habit even to our personal lives too. Here is how...

Most of us live in nuclear families these days. With many of us being working couples, we have no choice but to leave the kids on their own at times. As a consequence, when the kid raises his demands for something we go ahead and fulfill it. And I can see many more reasons for doing the same. First and foremost, we have the monetary empowerment. Secondly, we don't want to upset the kid. Last but not the least, we cleanse our guilt (of not having enough time to spend with them). Yet, we must stop this act of compensation.

As kids learn their basic values from their family, they must know how a 'no' looks and feels like—from none other than us. They must realize that the external world will subject them to much neglect and harshness. So it is better that they get their act right, when the time is on their side. But how can they execute it, if they don't even watch it being practiced at their homes? If each of their demands is met, they will lose the charm as well as the value of getting it. Take my son for instance. He keeps demanding for a new 'Wii' game every now and then. But, my declaration is clear and firm: only one per month is allowed. Though yes, abiding by this rule doesn't always produce a great feeling. It is tough to see our own son upset about something that we can easily afford. He gets upset when he sees his friends playing with all those new games. At the same time, there is a good part too! He thoroughly enjoys the game that he buys every month. Because he knows his dad won't comply, so he'd better enjoy what he has! And that is what he does. Moreover, he looks forward to the next month with great enthusiasm and in huge anticipation—valuing thus, whatever he gets. It is quite apparent from the way he selects his next month's 'goodie' on his iPad, and adds it to his wish-list.

By the way, the concept of wish-list reminds me of another great learning that life has to offer: God created this concept to let people know, *good things come to those who wait.*

One of the unsaid rules of my wife for our son is: "We will say 'no' to everything, which is unreasonable." If his demands are reasonable, we fulfill them even if that takes some time. But if they belong to the 'other side,' he knows our answer beforehand. Sometimes he cries and throws tantrums, but we turn a deaf ear—although it hurts within. After some time though, when he finds that he is not going to win, he returns to his original happy self. Both of us are very attentive towards how his character is shaping. We want him to pick up the habits which would instill the right kind of values in him, and stand him in good stead in the long run. When the stakes are so high, we know it is perfectly fine to say 'no' now, rather than the world saying a 'no' to him later. He is too young to understand the importance of all this now. But I am sure he will appreciate its value when he grows up.

Coming to the end of this chapter I share a great quote, as it upholds the context of the chapter:

> ***"I cannot give you a formula for success. But I can give you one for failure, which is: try to please everyone."***
>
> **Mark Twain**

Incidentally, this quote has found a permanent place on the wall of my office cabin.

4 Gold Standard

One day, I received a note of appreciation from one of my clients for working very hard on their assignment. The subject of his e-mail read: "You have set a Gold Standard!" Far from being flattered, I felt satisfied and happy that I was catering well to the customers and thus, was responsible for increase in the loyalty of customers towards my company.

Till this day, I remember the day when I was entrusted with this tough and demanding assignment. It came with a lot of baggage: tough and demanding customer, complex applications, stringent SLAs (service level agreements), high attrition, and delivery issues (the code which was being delivered had too many defects). Customer satisfaction was at an all-time low; yet, after only two years the same client sent this e-mail. Only I know the price I had to pay for this e-mail. When people came to know about it they flocked around, and asked the inevitable question: "What did you do differently?" They thought as if I had taken some magic potion prepared by the village druid Getafix, just the way he prepares for Asterix. Well, the answer was simple: hard work and nothing else. Some of the other factors that went in my favor, were: proactive communication, truthfulness, transparency, commitment and doing the right thing(s).

The most important factor that creates a difference in the lives of your customers, is your dedication. Sometimes you may get away with minor slips and misses, here and there. However, please be aware that your customers are not idiots. They are far more intelligent than you can ever imagine. They can judge the levels of your commitment and dedication, sitting thousands of miles away from you. There was one such client manager who had this unique ability to sense what others were doing, while on a teleconference. He knew exactly when we were listening to him and when we were not. He even coined the term, 'single tasking.' He would always tell his team in India, "When you are with me on phone, I want you to adopt 'single tasking,' which means: you are to do nothing else but hear me out." Whenever I called him, I ensured that I had no distraction(s). He demanded quality time and I always supplied the same.

The next in line is your ability to be truthful and transparent, as much as possible, with your customer(s). This includes, pro-active sharing of the problems that you face 'on the ground' and the way you deal with them. Furthermore, this implies that you must actively involve them in resolving the issues and bring the proposed solutions on the table, so as to allow them to have a 'sneak peek.' As one of my mentors always says, "In order to get the best out of your customers, try and get their skin into the game. Involve them. Make them a part of the process. Show them what you are doing and ask, whether they like your ideas. You must never treat your customers as aliens. Be transparent with them even when the going gets tough. A beating for the time being is better than getting killed forever." And Jack Trout terms this as 'one-to-one marketing.'

Moreover, I have seen that many managers try to avoid discussing the elephant in the room. They are more interested in discussing cats and mice. One of my colleagues was pretty good at it. He used to call this, 'deflection by choice.' The basis of his theory was: "Most of the executives from the client's side meet me once in a month. All I do is, spend more time on areas which have been running successfully—all the while trying to avoid discussions around important issues. Once the allotted time is over, you have successfully pushed the dot to the next month. Next month means 30 days, which is hell of a time for me to recover." I am not sure if he remained in business for long. Good luck to him!

We all love and adore fire-fighters. Right? But some people take the concept of fire-fighting to a different level altogether. They would first wait for the fire to start and expand, and then, like Ethan Hunt (the protagonist in the famous movie series, is a senior field operations agent for the IMF, an elite, top-secret espionage and covert operations agency that handles dangerous and highly sensitive international missions that have been deemed 'impossible') of the *Mission Impossible* series, would jump in to douse the flames. They sit tight until there is an explosion, and jump into action only when there is utter chaos with everyone running helter-skelter. This reminds me of another person: a perfect example for this situation...I always saw him in action when there was fire. It is a different story though, that most of his projects were always on fire! I never saw him reaching out to his customers when the going was good. In his world, having no fire would mean that all is *not* well. Good luck to him as well!

Another category of people that I have come across are infected with what I term, 'Struthious attitude.' Let me explain this syndrome first. When an ostrich (the only living member of the genus, Struthio) senses danger, all he does is puts his head into the sand and starts believing that the danger is no longer there. I know this is more of a myth, especially after Pliny the Elder (AD 23–79) wrote: "Ostriches imagine that when they have thrust their head and neck into a bush the whole of their body is concealed." And so, even if it is a myth, it explains my point well. This category would not spring into action even when they see fireworks in one of their projects. They would pretend as if everything is going well and will let their direct reports handle it. They are master practitioners of the religion: 'delegation.' Most of the times, they would practice downward delegation but sometimes, I have even seen them adopting upward delegation. They will effortlessly delegate it to their bosses and leave it to them to handle, and this they will do in such a way that makes it impossible to make out the 'real thing.' They would spin a plot, tell you the story like a showman, and declare as if everything is under control (of their poor direct reports) or out of control (which means, they want their boss to pitch in). If you have assigned *this* category of account executives to work for your clients, then better start counting backwards for the D-day. Your legal team will share the bad news soon.

One of the characteristics of the people belonging to these various categories, is their inability to assess the IQ levels of their customers correctly. An error that people make is, they put all their money on the 'relationship card.' Relationships do help in dousing the sparks before they become flames. But they can never be the substitute for fire-engines, equipped with the fire-fighting instruments: truthfulness, transparency, commitment and hard work. Playing with your customers is very similar to playing with the law. No matter how hard you try at playing, "Catch me if you can," you will ultimately be caught.

In my world, a brilliant client executive is the one who always reaches out to his customers pro-actively, and then like a smart doctor, diagnoses and treats the ailments early in the cycle before they turn into tumors. He would always act as a balm to their pains. Once you see this happening within your organization, sit back and relax. Very soon, your clients will entrust them with a 'family physician's' tag. *Let us not forget that a happy customer is a loyal customer.*

Talking about customer loyalty, this chapter is summed up by what **Allan Katz** (author, *Building Successful Client Relationships*) has to say on this subject:

> "One marketing mistake many retailers make is not doing anything to recognize their best customers. One of the best things you can do to create loyalty is to reward customers for shopping with you."

In my IT world, the reward for such customers could be in the form of giving them differential treatment, sealed by our commitment and truthfulness.

5 Don't be a Dinosaur

♣

One of my all-time favorite movies has been *The Jurassic Park* series. Every time it is screened on TV, both of us (me and my son) are glued to the TV set, yelling for popcorns. One of the main reasons for watching the same is the fact that I look forward to the great questions my son throws at me: "How many types of dinosaurs?"; "How long did they live?"; "What did they eat?"; "How big were they?"...and the like. I have always encouraged curiosity in kids. So, here we were, driving back home from a special screening of a movie (of the same series) in a theatre, when my son asked me, "Dad, where have all the dinosaurs gone now? Why can't we see them in zoo? Who killed them all?" Since it was a long drive, I answered all his questions in detail. I told him about the 'Ice Age' and their inability to cope with the change, as a result of which they became extinct. Though he did not appear to be too convinced with the reason forwarded, as he got an answer nonetheless, he tuned-in to his favorite music station—leaving me immersed in my own thoughts.

This whole episode reminded me of one of my favorite teachers (you rarely get such teachers these days) who always laid stress on the importance of adapting to the environment in which we live.

Since my father had a transferable job, my education went for toss periodically. It so happened that we landed at this small town, with a very basic school. When my father met the principal of the school he was told that physics teacher was not available there. Hence we had no option, but to opt for biology—at least for one year. This was tough for me for two reasons: I had left biology two years back; and I had no interest in the subject. But with no other alternative, my father just went ahead and got me admitted to this school. With great difficulty I somehow passed the exam and felt relieved. Little did I know that I was about to face a bigger problem in the next few days! Ever since my father arrived in this village (I wouldn't call it a city), he was constantly on the lookout for an opportunity to move to a bigger city, so that I could get the right kind of exposure needed at my age. And finally, he succeeded! He got a two-year posting in an urban city, which had the very best of schools. As I had picked up the habit of reading books at a very young age, it always came in handy. It helped me 'crack' the written exam and 'clear' the interview easily. Since I was always inclined towards engineering, I opted for physics again, dropping biology at the first opportunity! Anyone who has had a romantic stint with physics in his life, would agree that the subject is more conceptual than theory. If you don't get the concepts right at the very beginning, it would be better to change lanes. A gap of one year, and frequent change of schools, had drained me completely and rendered me clueless. Within the span of one year I had forgotten the concepts and thus found it very difficult to pick up the same again. The result: I flunked in my first term exams, with very poor score in physics. The physics teacher knew 'my history' very well (since my father had requested him personally to pay extra attention) and hence, he extended his full support.

Given that I had fared very well in all other subjects, the matter went to the principal and I was called in. On entering his cabin I found him to be reasonably young (not like the conventional ones) and well-dressed.

He heard my story patiently and said, "You are a bright student and I expect nothing else than good marks from you. My school has a reputation and I always make sure that it is maintained. And you are the ones who help me achieve it. One of the things that you will always face in life is: surviving under diversity. Life will always throw challenges at you. So how would you overcome such challenges? A mandatory requirement for dealing with any challenge is your ability to deal with change. If you can't handle changes, then you won't be able to handle challenges either. In this school, you will see that teachers comprise all age groups. Yet, the ones that I personally hire, are great adapters. They are flexible enough to change as per the needs of the environment. Take the case of your computer teacher. When I hired him, he knew just one of the programming languages but was willing to learn when the need arose. A couple of years later, the world of computers changed and the language that he knew became obsolete. This was the test of his adaptability. Despite his age, he took evening classes to learn the new languages and later, encouraged me to include them in the school curriculum as well. The same thing has happened to you. The physics that you left an year ago, is no longer the same. Hence, you are now finding it hard to deal with this sudden change. Dealing with change is not a problem, as long as you know and acknowledge that you have to deal with it, and not run away from it. So from now on, do not get depressed when you see changes happening all around you. Embrace them, before they kick you out. Always remember the age old saying, *'While in Rome, be a Roman.'* It is your mantra of survival."

I thanked him, not for the time he spent with me but for the valuable 'life lesson' that he gave me that day. I am still in touch with him and ensure that I meet him whenever I travel to that city.

Back to *Jurassic Park*! The prime reasons forwarded by the research groups for the extinction of dinosaurs are: a large meteor like explosion, which rocked the earth and released harmful gases; changes in the eating habits of the dinosaurs; and their inability to adapt to extreme hot and cold weather conditions. Take the case of our daily lives. We encounter changes all around: prices change, our office policies change, our children change (remember the famous 'generation gap' excuse?), our industries undergo changes...and even our competition changes with time. With so many changes happening around, how do you ensure your survival? Answer is simple: *it starts and ends with your mind. The battles are fought—and won or lost—in the mind.* If we can train our mind to first acknowledge the change, and then guide it on ways to deal with the change, the human race will survive (and not become extinct as a dinosaur). If we read autobiographies of famous people, we will realize that it was their agility and ability to adapt to the changes, which set them apart. History is replete with stories of how large corporations became dinosaurs over time—simply because they could not sense the change approaching. The company, Digital Equipment Corporation (DEC), is one classic example. And more and more companies are getting added to this list very rapidly.

A few days after the *Jurassic Park* screening that we had been to, my son insisted upon going on a picnic—out of the town—which his school had arranged on demand. Since this was not for the entire school, we were not really convinced. So we negated his demand. My son continued to put up a fight, and when he found himself losing, yelled in frustration, "Daddy, don't be a dinosaur."

I was happy to see that he had picked up my explanation so well, but was surprised too, as he used it on me to start with! Anyways, we decided to reward him—for 'this' presence of mind that he showed—by permitting him to go.

6 Great Expectations

♦

This one is about my father—a workaholic—who served the Government of India prior to his retirement. He was calm, focused—and always 'to the point,' when he spoke. For this habit of his, my mom used to tease him, "I pray to God that I die on a Sunday so that you won't have to take a leave for me. And yes, to make life even easier for you, we will marry both of our sons on a Sunday."

Incidentally, her declaration came true as both of us actually got married on Sundays!

When I grew up, I realized that some of his peers had done better than him—both in terms of money and title. Yet, I always found my father unfazed by the same. He would treat his friends (who were now a level or two above in the professional hierarchy) with the same love and respect, without any envy. All along, I knew my father was a brilliant man (he got many awards for successfully completing complex projects, which his peers never even dared to take up) and I firmly believed that he deserved more than what he got. But the thing that used to upset me always, was his patience. I never saw him complaining about anything—be it matters related to family or profession. There were times when I simply looked at him and mused, "God, how can someone be so patient?"

Contrary to this, at times people would come to me and tell, "Boy, you should be proud of your father. He has the unique ability to draw blueprints for some of the most complex bridges (he was a bridge designing expert). Learn from him." And I would sulk silently, "If he is so good, why is he not paid like others? Can't he switch job and cash on this uniqueness? When will we get richer?"

Years passed by and I could never initiate this discussion with him. I waited for the right day...and one day it came by itself. It was my first day at the engineering college. While I was getting ready, my father offered to drive me to the college. As soon as we hit the road, he began, "Son, getting into college is just like getting into a new life—a life which is very different from that you had in school. You will have more freedom and flexibility; and can afford to lead a less disciplined life. And before you know, you will pass out and start earning for yourself. So, before you become independent I want you to know some of the qualities that you must always adhere to." I knew where this conversation was heading. He continued, "First and foremost, there is no substitute for hard work; there is nothing called luck, in day-to-day life. Hence, never put large stakes on your luck factor. Remember, luck always favors the one who is prepared. People who do not work hard, look out for such lame excuses—blaming everything on the lack of luck. If you work hard you will ultimately get what you yearn for, even if at times the results come late. Hang in there because the rewards *will* come."

Thus, he went on, "The second requirement, my son, is to learn the art of being happy and content with what you earn. Earning money is an addiction. The more you earn the more you get addicted to it. Being rich is not a crime, being discontented is. So it is very important for you to be happy—with who you are and what you are. Take pride in whatever you do. Enjoy your job thoroughly. Learn to romance with your job. My professional career began with a job which did not match my skills. I was more qualified. Still, I took it, because I wanted a job badly. I took pride in that petty job and worked very hard. Very soon, my supervisor recognized my capabilities and raised the bar. He pulled me out of this assigned role, and put me in a job for which I was under-qualified! I see most of the kids taking up a job based on how much it pays—without realizing, if they would really enjoy doing that work. I know you too will do the same. All I am saying is, enjoy doing what you are asked to do and in the process, if you are paid handsomely, treat it as a bonus. Remember what Mahatma Gandhi said: *"Find the purpose and the means will follow."* If you concentrate on taking care of this underlying truth for the rest of your career, you will do just fine."

We were approaching the college. But my father was in no mood to put brakes on this interesting conversation. He had always been very quiet. As a result, such a frank discussion came as a pleasant surprise to me. It looked to me as if he had waited for this special day, to bring forth such a topic. He continued, "The third prerequisite, and the last one on my list, is to work for honor and dignity. Always remember that we are 'service class' people. We don't have large bank balances. But let me tell you, I am very rich when it comes to respect. The only thing that I have earned in my 30 years of service, is a life full of honor and dignity. I never worked for money. I always worked for respect."

I knew my time had come, because this was one area which was difficult for an 18-year undergrad to fathom. In fact, it had haunted me for many years.

Yet, the dilemma still persisted, on whether to broach all that had been nagging me since long. Though my college was approaching fast, I finally took the risk and asked, "Dad, can I ask you something? How do you handle expectations?"

He asked, "Self or others?"

"Self," I replied.

He paused for a while and responded, "Well, the best way to handle one's own great expectations, is to have 'no' expectations at all."

I was surprised by the answer. Honestly speaking, I had expected a detailed explanation.

But just then he elaborated on it, saying, "It all depends on how close you want to be with the reality. According to me, having no expectation is the right way. If you can control 'this lever' in your life, you will end up being very happy and content. The root cause of all our ailments is expectations. I agree that as a humans being you can't control your urge to expect the moment you do something for someone. That is how the barter system started. You give something, and then expect something else in return. That is how the world runs today. I don't expect you to row against the tide all the time. But I recommend: swim along the shore, rather than swimming in the mainstream like others. Striking a balance while swimming, is the real key to success. Even our ancient manuscripts have emphasized on the importance of hard work, without worrying about the results. Results are nothing but a way to feed your expectations. Therefore, if you do not form expectations, you will not worry about results. And when you don't worry about results, you work at your absolute best—with a free and fearless mind."

We had arrived at the college gate, and he knew he had to complete this conversation. So he hastened, "Once you worry about results, you will worry about success or failure. Once you worry about failures, you will worry about risks. And once you start worrying about risks, you will limit yourself. You will limit your abilities to learn, accept new challenges, face new situations. Hence, new learning too are missed. And when your learning stops, you become obsolete. One last thing before we stop: *always try to be progressive*. You must look into the past *only* when you need to learn from the mistakes that you made. Use them intelligently enough to evaluate your performance(s) and to fine-tune your goals for the future. Remember, when you do more than what you are paid for, you will eventually be paid more for what you do. All the best!"

As I walked through the campus gate (in anticipation of being ragged), I thanked my father for sharing priceless piece of experience—and wisdom—which I promised to keep in my heart and mind forever. *It was from that day that my respect for him increased further.*

7 Living Life, One Day At A Time

♥

Let this chapter begin with an honest admission: I feel blessed to have met a lot of wonderful people—from all walks of life—who have been responsible for my social and corporate upbringing. And for that, I am grateful to all. Some of them were great leaders, while others have been true mentors. But before narrating the incident—the catalyst behind this chapter—I would like to share with you the reason we should search for mentors; and also my realization on how they are different from leaders.

The best explanation that I have been led to, till date, has been by S. Radhakrishnan: he has defined a *mentor* as *an evolved leader*, in his book, *Corporate Chanakya*. He states that a leader is a part of the process while a mentor only gives the directions. Mentor only shows the path to walk upon, while a leader will lead the way—by walking with you. There have been times in my life when I could not find a leader around me. But as I had mentors, I never experienced the void that their absence, otherwise, would have led me to feel.

Just like leadership, mentoring is a skill hard to come across. Sometimes, I feel that both leadership and mentoring are heavily misunderstood words in corporate circles. Every second person that you meet, wants to be a mentor or a leader, without even realizing whether the person has 'it' in him/her. Apart from having the right kind of experiences for dealing with difficult situations, a mentor should also have the ability to balance his thoughts, actions and emotions. A mentor should be able to give you the much needed time. Unless you give (and get) the right kind of attention, the relationship between a mentor and a mentee will never be fruitful. On a number of occasions I have come across people who declared that they intend to become mentors, but realized later that they just don't have the time which a mentee requires, and thus demands.

Getting down to brass tacks, one of the things that I unerringly do is call or meet my mentors on a regular basis and get their valuable inputs. I call this experience: 'personal rejuvenation.' Similar to an over-excited kid, who opens up his bag of toys—and shows all his toys to the visitors—I too pour everything out to them: good things that I did, mistakes I committed, what was killing me, my concerns, my curiosities and my frustrations.

In one of my earlier roles, I had taken up many additional responsibilities in a bid to quickly move up the 'chain.' I accepted everything that came to me, without even thinking whether it was strategic in nature—and more importantly, without asking myself: "Do I have the bandwidth to do all this? Will I be able to do justice to all the responsibilities that I am taking?" Very soon, the side effects started showing up everywhere—even back home. Things started cracking everywhere, setting into motion an even larger ripple effect. I started spending sleepless nights, trying to complete all the tasks that I had taken upon myself. In the process, my reputation started taking a hit.

One of the habits that I have imbibed from my wife is to pay full attention to the kid's questions, no matter how busy I am. Her logic is simple, facilitated by what she had read about some research in this regard. According to her, a child's memory is like a computer's 'ROM.' The questions that come to their mind, stay only for a definite time span. Once you miss that, it is highly probable that your kid will forget what he wanted to ask.

And it is *this* habit that stood me in good stead when I was in the throes of self-inflicted stress. One night, as I was busy wrapping up my tasks (my wife had announced the last and final call for dinner) my son approached me. Having no idea of my mental state, he asked, "Daddy, what is meant by a silver lining on a dark cloud?" As I endeavored to answer his question I found my own woes alleviating immensely.

While I answered his query to his satisfaction, I recalled what one of *my* mentors said about silver linings: "Silver lining is present in all types of clouds that float above us. But you can see them only when the cloud gets darker. The darker the cloud gets, greater is the shine that the silver lining begets. Some of the best things in life come in contrasts. Thus, behind each failure a success lies hidden. All you need is the brain of Indiana Jones, and you are through!"

After attending to my son's query—which served as the silver lining *for me*—I knew I needed a 'rejuvenation' session with my mentor. Hence, I called him up after dinner. After a few minutes of chitchat he was made aware of the reason of my call. I told him about my current situation and the stress it had brought. After listening to me patiently he said, "You have been trying to solve too many things at the same time. Here is the deal: *all* you have to do is, live your life one day at a time!"

That was it! I realized...he was right. Since I had gotten into too many things simultaneously, I was not able to do justice to most of them. He went on..."Some of the most successful people—cutting across various industries—have learnt the art of doing one thing at a time. And today, they have managed to create a large fan-following by simply sticking to this mantra."

The conversation got interesting as he explained further... "Recently, I read about the making of Burj Khalifa, the world's tallest man-made structure. When they started designing it, the architects thought it would be impossible to create a structure like the one they had envisioned. Do you know what they did? They simply divided the whole thing into many smaller milestones, and handled them one by one. They started from the unique structural system called the buttressed core—which consisted of a hexagonal core, reinforced by three buttresses that form a 'Y' shape—for laying down 100 kilometers of water pipes, to place 26,000 blocks of glasses in a way that we all are proud of. *A great work of art is nothing but smaller pieces put together in a unique manner.* Anything which looks complex at the beginning, would look simple, the moment you start considering it one piece at a time. It was because of this uniqueness that the design engineers could rotate the building 120 degrees—from its original layout—to reduce the impact of the prevailing winds."

He gave me another example and continued on this topic...

"Have you ever solved a 600-piece jigsaw puzzle? Picture this for a while: when you put all the pieces on the table, you really do not know where to start with, because they are all scattered and are very different from one another. But once you succeed in finding that 'one' corner piece, then by linking it with the rest—one piece at a time—you finally end up completing the whole picture. The puzzle no longer remains so, as you access its entire meaning. Likewise, always remember that life is nothing but a very large and complex jigsaw puzzle. Solve it just the way I told you and you will be happy."

After we ended our session, I knew I will have a good night's sleep after many nights—and that I did have indeed.

8 It is All about the Franchise and the Character

♠

We usually love to watch fantasy and magical depictions. And if it has Harry Potter and his friends in it, the entertainment quotient goes up automatically. Over these years, the *Harry Potter* series had become a part of our life. I had seen kids waiting eagerly—for weeks, and even months—for the forthcoming novels and movies of Harry Potter. Me and my son were no different. I still remember the instance when we saw the first *Harry Potter* movie. My son was around 3 years old, and we were in the United States during that time. Though I knew that my son wouldn't understand anything at his age, still, having read the novel I knew he would enjoy it—at least later, if not sooner. Years passed by and here we were, booking movie tickets—online—for the last one in the series! It was a mixed feeling, filled with the kind of anticipation that is experienced when you approach the end of an exciting novel, along with the sadness associated with its completion.

The newspapers and the media worldwide, covered the release of the movie extensively. They also captured the musings of the people, which were similar to ours: "What would happen to our lives without Harry, Ron and Hermione?" Around the same time, I happened to read one interview that had appeared in one of the leading newspapers. In that interview, Daniel Radcliffe alias Harry Potter, stated, "It is very important for me to remember that the fans would be screaming *even* for somebody else, had *he* got the part. It is not about me. It is about the franchise and the character." Brilliant observation, and since it came from a young kid like Daniel, I was all the more impressed with the way he handled the situation.

How many of us think that way? And how many of us carry out that kind of reality check every now and then? I have seen many people who have abused power, fame and money under the refuge of a character. That character—or franchise—could be from politics, religion, and even from our corporate world. Most of the time they have been successful in using and abusing the system—bending it to work as per their ways—without realizing that it was due to the power of the position that they held, and nothing else. They fail to understand, what young Potter realized so early, so well. He knew that the fame he got was not due to—and for—him, but for and due to the character that he had lived all these years. And soon, he could well be forgotten once the *Harry Potter* series ends (unless he finds another such type of a character to live in).

I recently read that the real estate prices of a city had gone down by 50%, within weeks of the death of one of the religious gurus who dwelled in that city. This proved that the real estate developers failed to foresee the obvious. It was the guru's aura that had prompted people to buy property in that town. Hence, the moment he passed away, the prices spiraled downwards.

In one of the companies I worked earlier, there was a senior official, infamous for his arrogance and rudeness. Since his immediate boss was based in another country, he had a free run. There was no one to check on his ways. His approach to most of the problems was very simple and two-fold: shout and accuse. And yet, he always expected us to praise him on his style of working and the ways he adopted to solve issues! The guy was sharp and knew exactly what he was doing. He knew how to take advantage of a situation, fully drenched in the power that his role offered him. He promoted all the wrong people—basically *his* men—to all key positions. When such an environment prevails at the workplace, you expect one of these two things to happen to you: either you start looking for options and change the company (which some of us did, including myself) or you become a sycophant becoming one with the environment, and *make* the most of the situation.

After a few months of such a free run—and its resultant mayhem—the management finally understood the mistake of having him on board and forced him to leave. I was relieved—as well as sad—to hear the news. Relieved, because justice had finally prevailed, and sad, because many of us had left the company only due to this guy's histrionics. We could—and in all probability, would—have stayed back, if the management had acted swiftly.

But then, we too had our opportunity to get back at him! On a weekend, some of the old chums decided to meet over dinner. Frustrated, most of us had left the same company. Hence, the purpose behind the dinner was quite predictable. ☺. We wanted to know all that had happened a few weeks back—from those who had stayed back and put up a strong fight. As our gossip was at its peak, we saw someone walking towards us. Guess who? He was none other than the same old 'senior official,' who had been expelled recently. He presumed that we would stand up to say hello and would offer him a seat, inviting him to have a drink with us. He was wrong. Most of us decided to ignore him and thus, behaved as if we did not recognize him at all.

There are many reasons for which humans show respect towards another human being. The reason could be: experience, knowledge, leadership qualities, seniority, power, helping attitude, etc. When these parameters were applied to *this guy*, he *failed* miserably in almost all the departments. He had lost the respect of his colleagues—juniors as well as seniors—as the only thing he had acquired was 'power' alias the 'franchise,' which was no longer with him. *And this, he realized the hard way.*

While he walked away, after being completely ignored, I learnt a lesson of life: *if you want to earn respect, don't expect the 'chair' or your 'visiting card' to do that job for you.*

9 Max Payne vs. Call of Duty

♣

One of my favorite past-times has been to indulge in video games, irrespective of their type. The genre could be action, simulation or strategy. However, I am addicted more to *FPS* (First Person Shooter) games.

And genes do speak! Years later, I find my junior equally crazy about them. In fact, he came out smarter than his dad in some of the games that we played. The time that I took to complete games like *Transformers*, *God of War* series, etc., was much more than what my son took! And in some of the cases, I didn't even teach him the 'controls.' He just picked—and mastered—them by the 'hit and trial' approach. Ever since I taught him to browse the internet, he has picked up the art of using 'cheat codes' to finish his games faster. I still remember the occasion when both of us played *Halo*, on our respective machines, and reached the last level of the game together. And both of us got stranded at one point—the same one—where the time to move out of the exploding ship was too less for us to get out safely and finish the game. It was a race against time, and no matter how hard we tried we failed again and again. But one evening, when I came back from the office, I found my son anxiously waiting at the door to break some news—good news, which it indeed was. He had completed the final level of the game in the interim! I asked him the trick and he proudly showed me how to do it. When I asked him about the source of his information, his answer surprised me with its simplicity: he had used the gaming forums to post the question, and one *Halo* fan showed him how to do it step-by-step. It amazes me whenever I see kids 'picking up' things effortlessly, and bringing in a fresh perspective, when it comes to resolving difficult situations; and this incident reinforced the amazement.

It was one of those times of the year when both of us were eagerly awaiting the release of two new games. One was from the *Rockstar Games*, and the other from *Activision*. We knew we would ultimately end up playing both the games. But the question was: which one to try first...*Max Payne vs. Call of duty or Black Ops*? My son declared, "Let's try *COD* first (*Call of duty* is referred to as *COD* by its fans worldwide)." I asked him the reason for his choice and his instant reply came: "*COD* gives me an opportunity to play in teams. We cannot always accomplish the various missions assigned to us without the help of our fellow teammates. I feel happy when I have to lead a team of soldiers and guide them through a mission successfully. In some of the missions, I also get an opportunity to play like a 'Private,' and take orders from my seniors to complete the various tasks assigned. However, when it comes to playing Max Payne, I have to do everything by myself and that gets very boring at times." That was indeed a thoughtful and brilliant observation by my son.

When I introspected on his observation further, I realized that it fitted so well in our corporate lives as well. Whether we agree or not, but the *truth of the hour is: the days of individual players are over*. Most of the organizations prefer team players: people who can play within teams and deliver. I had discussed this aspect with lot of HR experts and friends, and they too believe that people who can work in teams are better at helping others. Furthermore, they are able to attain the collectively set goals, without worrying about anything else.

One of my HR director friends shares this passion—for teamwork—appropriately, "I will give you a very easy way to select the right kind of candidates for any role that you might be hiring. Try and ask questions which places the candidates in situations where the choice is between 'I' (as an individual) and 'O' (as in ours). If you see them putting the 'I' before 'O,' then they are not welcome in the current organization setup. Bid them goodbye very politely."

As a matter of fact, I myself have made it very clear to my hiring teams on this account. My one-line directive to them has been: "Filter out team players and ensure that we don't hire individual contributors." I have advised them to design a set of questions which can help to spot and weed out such people, right at the hiring stage. Even for people who have already been in the organization, team-playing skills must be an important prerequisite for them to be promoted. And if an organization can ensure putting great team players at the top, I assure you, the results that flow would be beyond their imagination.

Working in teams is very important for collective success. Such people become great managers down the road. They handle people's aspirations deftly. They understand people's issues better. They always think about meeting the team's goals, rather than worrying about their individual KRAs (key result areas). They turn out to be better decision-makers, with their decisions reflecting care and a personal touch—the two main ingredients in the recipe of success, for any 'human capital' based organization.

A quote by **Harry Truman**, read long ago, still reverberates in the mind:

> "It is amazing what you can achieve and accomplish if you do not care about who gets the credit."

10 | Did you Get Hurt?

♦

One afternoon, I got a call from a very good friend of mine. We had worked together for years in the past, and since then we had kept in touch. While I am 'the practical' sort of a guy, he is more of an emotional person. He had not been keeping well and was at home, recuperating. Thankfully, he recovered and resumed his duties within a couple of weeks. But when he called, he was not in his usual mood. Since we knew each other well, it was easy for me to sense *that*. I asked him if there was something that bothered him. And then, hardly a few minutes into the conversation, he confessed, "You know what...I have been hurt. During the couple of weeks when I was seriously ill, my well-wishers and colleagues called me up to inquire about my health. One person, who did not even bother to ask about my well-being, was none other than my own boss. To be honest, I never expected such a behavior from him. After all, he banks so heavily on me. Yet, he did not bother to check even once?"

I consoled him saying, "Man, he must be busy and might have forgotten in the process. Give him the benefit of doubt and move on."

But he was inconsolable and continued, "No, he wasn't that busy. He did call me thrice during this phase. But all that he discussed was work. He simply did not care to ask about my health." However, we ended the conversation, with his boss finally being given the benefit of doubt.☺.

This incident immersed me in a deeper thought.: at times, we become so busy with our routine jobs that we fail to reciprocate with seemingly small acts of love, compassion and gratitude. We forget the basic principles on which humanity functions: to care about others, and help them when they are in need. Is it that difficult? After all, the investment that I am talking about is nothing more than a few minutes of ours every day. These minutes could be used for making quick calls and sending a few messages to all those who need them the most—*when they need them the most.* It could be your long-lost friend, with whom you had not connected for years; it could be your cousins, your uncle, aunts, your teachers—and even your neighbors. Yet, we always pretend to run short of those few minutes or act miserly, while spending them. We must realize that those few seconds do reflect a lot of our qualities: how we care for others; how much importance do we give to relationships and thus, how we treat our relations; and what does friendship mean to us.

Furthermore, there could be another facet to it altogether. Sometimes we don't even consider it as an important activity. But it doesn't mean that we are careless. It is just that we simply fail to notice its importance, at times. Maybe, that was the reason why we both decided to give the benefit of doubt to his boss. And yes, fortunately *I* had 'messaged' him twice, to check on his health—without even realizing that had I not sent those messages, I too would have hurt him, even if unintentionally.

So next time, when you see your friends or relatives in pain and suffering, simply pick up the phone and call or send a message. Show them that you care.

And remember, while it may not cost you more than a few cents, it is priceless to the person who receives it.

Come on... Let us respect humanity.

11 Have You Trained Your Commanders Well?

♥

A lot of people have shared a common frustration with me: "I want to do more than what I am doing but I don't know how to." The first question that I ask them is, "Have you trained your commanders well?" And most of the time, I get an ambiguous response, "Yes. I have delegated enough work to them. Some of my direct reports are not capable of handling more than what they are doing. My managers are great, but they are frustrated as well. So how can I convince them to take up more?"

This brings me to one of the most common perceptions that we all carry while addressing the issue. Most of us believe that to develop the next line of commanders (a term which I have used to represent the direct reports), all that we need to do is, delegate more to get our job done. Well, it is easier said than done! By delegating effectively, we address only half the issue. There is a lot more to it which needs our attention. Let us not forget the time that we need to invest in mentoring and nurturing them. After all, we need to water our crops regularly—in addition to using a good mix of high quality manures—to ensure a rich harvest.

But then, why is it important to develop and train your commanders well?

Well, the benefits of having a strong and competent line of commanders are immense. First obvious benefit, which is the easiest to understand: it frees you and gives you more bandwidth to take up newer roles and challenges. It simply empowers you to accomplish more, with the same set of routine eight hours' work each day that we all are allocated. It enables you to focus on the core issues and challenges that demand your attention. And all this while, you are confident that the less important tasks are being taken care of by your commanders. This allows you to devote your full attention—and put in your best—towards solving the critical ones.

According to an old maxim: *giving a man a fish may feed him for a day, but teaching him how to fish will feed him for lifetime.* Therein lies the second reason: your commanders must feel that they are being constantly developed in the process. So here is the deal: while you see this process as an investment from your side, similarly, they too must view their choice—to spend time with you—as a wise investment of *their* time. Otherwise, why would they? Research has proven that humans feel satisfied when the process involves some sort of theoretical or practical learning. If your commanders get the feeling that all that they do is carry out your orders, without getting any opportunity to apply their own intelligence at all, then the good ones will surely run away. And you will be forced to go back to where you started from: *find a replacement and train them.*

We need to understand that there is a fine line of demarcation between 'proper delegation' and 'effective delegation'—the two terms that are used in the context of 'delegation.' Most of the time, we delegate tasks like approvals related to administrative affairs, where there is either no risk or very little risk involved (read: proper delegation). However, the truth is, we need to ensure that we delegate the right tasks.

I remember reading an article about a gang of robbers who had created a lot of trouble for the local police. When they were finally caught after months of toil, the police found: the leader of the gang used all gang members effectively, by rotating their jobs (thus making it difficult for the police to nail any one of them based on the specificity of their work). Furthermore, they shared the booty equally, and not according to their jobs. I know, using the workings of a gang of robbers to describe the situation is a bad example to extend. Yet it is being forwarded, as it brings out two relevant aspects to ponder on:

- All members of the gang were treated equally, which meant that they were delegated with all types of jobs—even though the risk of getting caught was high due to their inadequate experience in every domain. The leader of the gang still went ahead and took the risk.
- They shared the booty equally, making each gang member feel as if he were the leader.

This is what we need to do, as far as effective delegation is concerned. Delegate those tasks which will help them to develop over the years—the ones that will enable them to move up the 'value chain.' Assign them the tasks where there is an opportunity to make mistakes, so that they learn in the process—tasks, which when completed, give them satisfaction and thus make them feel great and proud of themselves. And once your commanders realize their capabilities, they will become far more effective than you can even think of.

This brings me to the third reason, which is an extension of the second and answers one of the other commonly asked question: "Even after delegation, why am I not able to find time for the right work?" The answer lies again in the art of practicing effective delegation. Only effective delegation will free your 'real' bandwidth, and make you more productive in the process. And once your 'real' bandwidth is freed, you could take up those 'satisfying challenges'—those which always made to the list, but never made to the table.

Here is another benefit of practicing effective delegation, which is slightly strategic and its fruits are borne in the long run. It will help you to take your legacy to multiple levels—rendering it all-pervasive—in your organizational setup. Let me elaborate upon this a bit more. When you have a small team, it is very easy to instill a culture of disciplined, definitive working style; strong operating principles; and good working habits at all levels because you can choose to spend time with most of them personally.

However, when your team grows and becomes large, you lose that personal touch over time. The only way to keep that 'touch of yours' alive is through your well-trained team of commanders, who align with your thought process and vision. And this you can achieve only if you delegate the right tasks and thus, enable your commanders to learn and pass your legacy at all levels effortlessly—resulting in creation of a highly effective and productive organization.

One of the great rulers in Indian history, Emperor Akbar, was not literate. But he had this unique ability to choose the best generals that history could produce. No wonder, he was one of the greatest Mughal rulers of all times and was widely famous for his principles around justice, equality and religion.

Regarding effective delegation, one of my mentors used to tell me, "By practicing effective delegation you can be one hundred percent sure that *even after your retirement* you are remembered for the right reasons. You can rest in peace when you know that your blood and sweat did not go waste. Most of the times, the head of the company does not train any of his commanders—well enough—to take his place when he is no more. Gone are those days when the eldest son used to be an automatic choice. The Wall Street days are ruthless, and unless you put the right successor at the helm, you are signing upfront for failure. The only way to avoid such failures: choose a commander, and train the chosen one by delegating the most complex challenges to him—for resolution—while he is still under your hood."

I remember what **Booker T. Washington** once said so brilliantly:

> ***"There are two ways of exerting one's strength. One is pushing down, and the other is pulling up."***

So work towards 'pulling up' as many people working for you as possible, and see how that frustration and de-motivation dissipates at all levels within your organization.

"Develop downwards, to move upwards!" This one is from me.☺.

12 Have We Forgotten "Him"?

♠

One day, while driving to the office I took a different route—the one longer than the one I usually take—as I had a brief meeting over breakfast with a person en route to my office. The meeting went off well and thereof I headed for my office. During that drive something happened, significant enough, to force its way out in the form of this chapter.

There is a major traffic signal on this route: pretty long, almost a three-minute stop. While I waited for the light to turn green, I noticed a family of five, sitting on the pavement. The family, consisting of a mother and her four kids, appeared to be very poor and homeless. The eldest one might have been around twelve years old; the second one, around eight; the third hovering around five; and the youngest, not more than 3 years of age. The youngest, and the one immediate senior, hardly wore anything and the other two too, were scantily dressed. The mother was no better than her children. The clothes she wore seemed to be torn at multiple places. It was obvious that they were extremely poor, and begging was their means to make their ends meet.

The mother sat on one side, and with her four kids facing her they made a circle—with a bowl placed in the middle. Even the bowl was partly broken. It contained either rice or porridge—it was difficult to ascertain from the distance. Sitting in the car, I could sense that the mother and her kids were about to eat something for their breakfast. The kids seemed to be disciplined and caring. The eldest sat beside the youngest so that he could help him grab a few bites. Just when they were about to start, their mother stopped everyone and told them to pray. At this, all of them folded their hands and started praying along with their mother. I was touched to see that despite leading such a tough life, with so little to eat and almost nothing to wear, the mother and her kids did not forget to thank the Almighty first—for *whatever* they had. They exhibited restraint. In spite of being very hungry they prayed first.

By the time the signal turned green, the family had started eating together, with the mother still helping the youngest one to eat. The mother had not eaten, till the time my eyes could see them—courtesy, the rearview mirror.

As I drove, on my way I thought:

- In this fast moving life, how many of us take the time to thank "Him" for being with us?
- When a family, living in such deplorable state, could think about "Him," why can't we?
- Why do we remember "Him" only when the going gets tough or when something is not working or when we want something?
- Why do we have to remember "Him" only when someone is admitted in the intensive care unit?
- Why do we have to remember "Him" before the exams, and not earlier?
- Why can't we thank "Him" every day, for all that "He" does for us?
- Why do we behave with "Him" as in a barter system—since we remember "Him" or thank "Him" only when we achieve or accomplish something?

These questions need to be answered. We simply cannot run away from them... So long we do, we will be chased by these questions. But if we sincerely search for the answers and accept them honestly—as and when they come up—we will be guided to the needful...and with it, to a peaceful life.

Before I forget, let me admit that I took the same route next morning too—not to attend any meeting this time, but to donate clothes and a few packets of rice to this very 'special' family.

13 Eat that Frog!

♣

This chapter is inspired by the precious knowledge that I gained from Brian Tracy's book, *Eat That Frog!*

There is an old saying: "If the first thing that you do when you wake up in the morning is eat a live frog, then nothing worse can happen for the rest of the day!"

In his bestseller, Brian Tracy states that your 'frog' should be the most difficult item on your 'to do' list—the one you're most likely to procrastinate on. Because if you eat that first, you will be energized and gain momentum for the rest of the day, as it no longer comes in the way.

I completely agree with Brian. At times, our basic human nature forces us to 'push back' the most difficult or ugly task (the frog) as much as possible. Because of it, we end up doing two things: we spend time with tasks lower in priority, and we compromise on productivity. Suppose, we decide to let the frog (the most difficult task) lie on our plate, while we order a few delicacies (easier and cosmetic tasks) for ourselves. No matter how hard we try to relish the delicacies, the mere presence of the frog—lying stale on the plate—will stop us from enjoying the delicacies to the fullest.

I recall one such incident when one of my business unit (BU) owners wanted me to meet few dissatisfied managers of his team. The reasons for their dissatisfaction were varied.

I have always encouraged transparent communication through

frank discussions within my group, as I always appreciate heart-to-heart dialogues. It is very important to meet dissatisfied people in our teams. But it doesn't mean that we have to meet them *only* when we have a solution to their issues. The mere acknowledgement of the issues also helps to relieve the burden that people carry in their hearts.

According to my BU owner, this case—of one particular dissatisfied manager—was a difficult one to handle. Let us call this person Mr. A. We had spent a lot of time on Mr. A, addressing his issues and concerns. However, he still refused to understand and threatened to quit. He was critical of my customers and business. Hence, we knew that we would have to handle him delicately. While giving the list of all such folks, my BU owner suggested: "You need to spend time with all of them and help me retain them within the group. And yes, please take special care of 'this one' (Mr. A). Since he is going to take a lot of your time and energy, I would recommend taking him up last."

You know what I did? I went ahead and did exactly the opposite. I set up a meeting with Mr. A the very next day, having decided to eat the frog lying on the plate first. Not because he was overtly critical (which in any case, all of them were) of my business, but because he was the most difficult of all.

I must admit that the meeting was indeed a tough one. But what is more important is the outcome: once I was through with the meeting, I felt relaxed and easy. It looked like I had all the time in the world now to take care of the other tasks at hand—since the most difficult one on my list had been already taken care of.

Hence, the next time you have to 'eat that frog,' do it right away, over breakfast...and enjoy your lunch and dinner, savoring many delicacies!

P.S. Mr. A went on to work with me for a few more years after that meeting of ours.

14 You are Not Immortal!

♦

One morning, as I woke up and grabbed the newspaper, one of the headlines in the 'business section' attracted my attention: "Apple ends Nokia's 15-year smartphone reign." I was not surprised though. All along these years, I had been using Nokia phones, just like my friends did. However, this headline reminded me how each one of us had lately shifted our loyalty from Nokia to other prominent brands: Samsung, HTC, BlackBerry and Apple.

There was a time when Nokia was the undisputed leader in the cellular phone market. It was during the same time that most of the leading journals and magazines covered the success story of Nokia. There were full page articles on how it had emerged and established itself as the leader in all major categories of cellular phones, be it the smartphones or the touch phones. Furthermore, history was made in 2006, as Nokia crossed the unprecedented sales figure of a billion handsets.

And that was the anticlimax in the saga of Nokia's journey—as something else unfolded. This milestone made Nokia executives crown themselves as God of the cellular phone market. They started believing that 'they were immortal' and hence, nobody could ever kill them in the arena of cellular phones.

If you have read D'Allesandro and Jack Trout extensively, you will realize that this is one of the biggest mistakes that market leaders have made in the past as well. In fact, it has been one of the main reasons for extinction of some of the most prominent brands ever. Such a thought process had made them overconfident and thus, careless. And when you become overconfident, you start making decisions based on your inflated ego, instead of applying logic and utilizing objectivity.

In this entire process, Nokia had to pay heavily: for their decision to leave the US market, their decision to stick to their own Symbian platform, the delay in releasing dual SIM mobile phones (especially in India and Southeast Asian countries), etc. They also stuck to their strategy of keeping their product-line small, introducing new models at a very slow pace. All these moves dealt multiple blows to the major market share that they held—both in the smartphone and 'dumb phone' categories. Some of its competitors were fast to adopt an open platform for developing their products, thus, giving the freedom and flexibility to their customers to benefit from the open source industry. And still others, went the 'touch' way to come out with innovative features, which were unthinkable on a Nokia handset.

As an icing on the cake, they injected new models in the market at such a fast pace that it affected a large portion of Nokia's share. Even the Chinese and the Southeast Asian countries took advantage and bombarded the market with cheap dual SIM phone sets, which were hard to resist. All these ate into Nokia's share in the cellular phone market. Consequently, its hold weakened in the arena of cellular phones.

Another player came out with the concept of an 'App World,' to take advantage of this situation. It offered the customers a unique way to shop for their music and other software and utilities. As a niche player, Apple thus entered into the professional smartphone category, and took away even a large share of Nokia's corporate customers. Before Nokia could realize what was happening, its game was over. They had landed themselves in a position where they not only lost customers (having failed to listen to the voice of the customers and realize their power), but more importantly, they lost their own credibility—the promise and belief that the Nokia brand once stood for. They failed to realize that a brand has to live within its perceptive world which gets created over the years. The moment you step out, you are a dead fish!

While more on the importance of deftness follows in one of the later chapters, I wanted to draw your attention to some of the other factors that we must always be attentive to.

When we climb up the corporate ladder we must never let overconfidence creep into our mind. Treat it as the *only* recipe for failure. Our decisions must be taken after a thorough and diligent assessment, exhibiting logic and objectivity thus. We must never assume that our customers do not have a choice, and that they won't run away from us. Remember the carving on the stone: "We all have choices." Therefore, special emphasis should always be laid on the competitive landscape—and on our own position with respect to the same. We need to keep assessing, day in and day out, whether our brand is delivering the value and promise it stands for.

In accordance, I sum up this chapter with a beautiful quote from my favorite author:

> *"Arrogance is the first sin. It works like this: success often leads to arrogance and arrogance leads to failures."*

Jack Trout

Brand strategist and Guru

15 Rise Like a Phoenix!

♥

As we were about to hit the bed one night (we are morning birds, so we sleep pretty early by Indian standards), my cell phone rang. It was an unknown number and before I could ignore it, my son picked it up and said, "Hello! Who is it?" And there I was, left with no choice but to take the call.

At the other end of the line was a very old acquaintance. Actually, he used to work for me once upon a time. On hearing his voice, the past few years flashed in front of my eyes... I could visualize him, standing in front of me and instantly I was transported to the past...

He had been working for the organization long before I joined the same. Since we worked with different departments, we simply knew that we existed within this company and shared a great 'hi-hello-how-are-you in-the-corridor' kind of relationship. Over the years, I came to know that his career had not progressed well. Although, I didn't know the reason(s) behind it. And then, one fine morning he was transferred to my team. We started off well and I told him to forget the past (one of the prerequisites for working with me is to have an 'always look forward' attitude). I acknowledged that a few things indeed had not gone well in his previous assignment. Hence, my suggestion to him was to use those experiences as learning from the past and start afresh.

A few months later, he started doing well and established himself. My job was done. I always ensure that I give enough time to all who join me at the senior most level, so that they can settle down nicely in a new setup. And once they start performing, I leave them pretty much on their own—just like the mother bird allows her young chicks to exercise their freedom to fly and explore the world around. I hardly interfere, unless they approach me for help and guidance.

Few months later, he sent me an e-mail seeking an appointment. When we met, he disclosed that he wanted to move on—to newer pastures and explore fresh avenues. He confessed that though he was happy with his current job profile, he wished to switch jobs as his past continued to haunt him. Some of the opportunities that he had pursued, before joining my team, had materialized and he wanted to make use of them. I spent some quality time with him, and explained how he must use the opportunities being provided to him in his current role in the company—to showcase his skills and climb up the 'ladder of success.' Since I could foresee a bright career for him within the current setup, I tried my level best to dissuade him from changing jobs.

Anyways, after a number of meetings we decided to part ways amicably.

After he left we kept in touch for a few months—and after that left it on LinkedIn to keep us connected!

This forms the backdrop to the phone call I had to take that night.

On hearing his voice after so many years, I started off by asking how he was and how was his family doing. His tone was low, and clearly conveyed that he was not happy about something.

Soon, he came to the point and blurted: "Boss, I am not doing well at all. But the reason for disturbing you so late in the night is the fact that I wished to confess something."

I was confused, since we had actually parted ways on a good note.

He went on... "All these years, ever since I left you I could not settle down. I made the wrong choices and took lot of wrong decisions."

I interrupted and corrected him, "They were simply bad decisions." (In my dictionary, there is nothing called right or wrong; it is always good versus bad.)

"Yes, they were bad decisions. I changed companies too frequently and worked in various cities, leaving my family behind. I even changed my profile and role...but nothing worked. I felt like I was going down and down—caught in a whirlpool. And the more I tried to come up, the faster I was pulled down.

I have faced such immeasurable pains and huge failures in life that I cannot take it anymore. I am tired and completely broken. I feel like ending my life and be free...once and for all."

Before I could say something, he stopped me and pleaded that he be allowed to speak.

"Please let me continue, boss. For many years I did not have the guts to call you. There were many occasions, when I dialed your number. But before you could answer the call I hung up every time. Today, I have gathered a lot of courage to stand up and call you. All these years, at each such juncture when I failed, I was reminded of every word that you had uttered as you tried your level best to stop me from leaving the job and *your company*. I was so inebriated by my new offer letters that I completely ignored what you suggested—yet, only to remember it later...every other day. I have hurt you so much that till date I feel like I am getting it back. Please forgive me and release me from this guilt, so that I can concentrate on my life."

By now, I knew this was serious stuff. So I went to the living room, to continue with the call without disturbing others. Then I told him to calm down first.

But, after ending his monologue he broke down and began to weep. His pain was palpable and it was evident that he was going through a very tough phase in life—tougher than he could handle. I knew that if *I* did not handle the situation in the right manner, I could lose him for life.

I told him to forget the past and start concentrating on the future. I asserted that life has good things in store *for all of us*. And to rid him of his guilt (which in any case was absolutely uncalled for) my discourse began...

"To be honest, I have never thought bad about you. So, the question of your asking forgiveness does not arise. You had choices to make and you just picked those which you thought were the best. We all do that. While making a choice, we hardly know the direction it will ultimately lead us to. But that is the fun part of it. If you know beforehand the consequences of a choice, how will you learn? It is like a leaked exam paper. You know the questions that would come, and you prepare accordingly to finally pass the exam with good marks. But you know what? When you come across an opportunity, that needs your skills and knowledge, you will never be able to apply that knowledge—as, it is not knowledge that is acquired thus; it is just an exam that is passed, that too, using a leaked exam paper. That is why it is always important to work for the unknown. When you work on areas where the results are a mystery, you will gain even if you fail.

You have encountered a series of failures which have made you emotionally weak—and nothing else. It is okay to come across failures in life. All you have to do now is, carry a postmortem of your past. *You should always use your past as a tool to calibrate your future.*

Remember, just like a phoenix we too must rise from the ashes, every time we get burnt by our decisions. We have to see these failures as opportunities to start afresh, and with heightened understanding of the situation."

Further to this, I gave him ideas regarding the persons he must meet, and the companies he must apply to. I also offered to thoroughly review his resume and make the necessary corrections. Overall, the next 30 minutes were devoted to boost his confidence, and providing him with the encouragement that he badly needed. I promised to call him weekly to keep track on how he was doing, and assured him that in few weeks' time he will land up at the right place. At the back of my mind, I knew that he had the right skills; and hence, was confident that once he crosses the man-made emotional barrier(s), he will emerge as a winner.

A few days later, while watching the third installment of *The Transformers: Dark of the Moon* with my son, I heard a beautiful line that Optimus Prime said to Sam. The line is absolutely *in line* with the context of the chapter:

> ***"There will be times when you will fail in whatever you do. Your friends will turn into enemies and the world will become a difficult place to live in; but do not give up your faith in yourself and everything will be fine again."***
>
> Optimus Prime, Chief of Autobots
> The Transformers

P.S. After a few weeks, this old acquaintance of mine got into one of the best companies and started off yet again, with a renewed vigor.

Note: Here are a few words on *The Transformers: Dark of the Moon*:

Optimus Prime is the leader of the Autobots, a faction of transforming robots from the planet Cybertron. The Autobots are constantly waging war against a rival faction of transforming robots called Decepticons. Prime is depicted as a brave, powerful, wise and compassionate leader who uses his talent to improve the universe around him and has dedicated himself to the protection of all life, particularly the inhabitants of earth. He is portrayed as having a strong sense of justice and righteousness.

Sam Witwicky is the human protagonist in the movie series.

16 Always Outnumbered, but Never Outmanned

♠

I am sure, by now all of you know about the best kept secret of my life: playing video games and be crazy like hell about them! It also happens to be one of the common passions that I share with my junior too.

One day, my son was watching one of the previews of the new game, *Medal of Honor*, on his iPad, when he came to me and said, "Dad, listen to what Dusty* says… *'I am always outnumbered but never outmanned.'* Isn't that a great line?"

I replied, "Son, it is a great line indeed and has a great underlying meaning too. While it is so true to the spirit of an elite commando, it also tells you about how you must react to life's unseen obstacles. Never be afraid of getting into tough situations. Fight them bravely just like Dusty does—fighting all the terrorists in the game."

He said, "Okay, dad," and went back to his iPad on which he watches all these videos.

However, it made me sink deep into my thoughts. Though the dialogue with my son had ended, its effect stayed because of the certain facts of life that it beheld so subtly. How many times has life thrown us into such seemingly difficult situations, where we start feeling as if we were being 'outnumbered' in fighting

---

*Dusty is a character in the game.

them? Innumerable!

In fact, that is how life treats us most of the times: so unpredictably. At times it is for the good, while sometimes it is even for the worse. But one thing that we all need to ensure, is to be never ever 'outmanned.' I remember reading an intelligent quote, which explains this beautifully: "Anyone can give up, and its the easiest thing in the world to do. But to hold it together, when everyone else would understand if you fell apart, that is true strength."

I have always been in agreement with this quote. Giving up, is indeed the easiest thing to do. Yet, we need to behave like Dusty who always stands up to fight against all odds. To fight without worrying about the consequences—whether we would emerge as victorious or be martyred—is an act of courage and confidence. To fight for the right cause, to fight for the team, to fight for the country (all of which Dusty does) is a fight for honor. And this is what matters in the end. It really doesn't matter whether we win or lose. Important is, whether we keep the spirit of 'never giving up' alive or not. What does matter is whether we could bring smile on someone's face, and whether what we did was correct or not. If your conscience comes up with a big 'yes,' agreeing with *all these that matter*, then give yourself a pat on your back—because you just 'outnumbered' your enemies.

While on this topic, I am also reminded of one of my favorite motivational dialogues from the movie *Karate Kid 2*. During the last few minutes, when Dre Parker (Jaden Smith) emerges as the winner against Cheng and goes to his teacher, Mr. Han (Jackie Chan), for his blessings, Han tells his favorite student, "Son, this is what *I learnt from you*. Life will bring you down a number of times. What matters is, whether we want to stand up again or not." Mr. Han truly belonged to the 'Dusty clan,' I must admit.

Another very powerful thought on this topic, which comes to my mind, is a quote by **Henry Miller** (famous American author). Though it is a long one, but when read with patience, its beauty will reveal itself to all.

Relish it...

"Life moves on, whether we act as cowards or heroes. Life has no other discipline to impose, if we would but realize it, than to accept life unquestioningly. Everything we shut our eyes to, everything we run away from, everything we deny, denigrate or despise, serve to defeat us in the end. What seems nasty, painful or evil can become a source of beauty, joy, and strength, if faced with an open mind. Every moment is a golden one for him who has the vision to recognize it as such."

Note: Here is more on Dusty, for those who are interested.
Belonging to the Tier-1, SFOD-D (Delta Force) unit, Dusty has a long thick beard, wears sunglasses and a baseball cap— backwards—which reads FDNY. He works for the AFO Wolfpack, which consists of himself and his mates: Deuce, Panther and Vegas.

17 Pride and Prejudice

♣

My 11-year old son wanted me to explain the term: prejudice. It had come up in the new chapter that was being taught in his class. My style of teaching has always been very different, and in accordance my directives have been: "Do not resort to cramming. Try to understand the concept, and use your own language to explain it when the teacher asks anything pertaining to the same." Therefore, he wanted me to give him some 'real life' examples—so that he would be armed well enough to field the questions in his class, the next day.

Hence, I started explaining, by giving him a number of examples on what prejudice is all about—and how, we as human beings, get prejudiced over time in dealing with life's situations. I gave him the examples of the manner in which many of us get prejudiced, courtesy: religion, economic status, language, the work that we do, the things that we eat, the clothes that we wear, the cars that we drive, the company that we work for, the school that we go to, the gadgets that we own, the colony where we reside, the city that we have settled in, and the like...as the list is actually endless.

Suddenly, he interrupted and said, "Dad, I have understood. Can I go now?" and before I could say, "Yes," he slipped away to his study table, to complete the rest of his daily assignments.

I usually get very passionate when I have to explain concepts to anyone and hence, get under the skin of the same. So I hardly realized how deep I had dived, while explaining what prejudice is. No wonder, he ran away in the middle of the conversation. ☺. Maybe, it was too much of a sermon for an 11-year old. But it left me, yet again, in the depths of my thought...on the topic.

It is interesting to observe how we change over a period of time and get accustomed to our surroundings—the one which is created by our society. We are being taught about 'prejudice,' right at the age of eleven. At the same time, we forget its real meaning as grown-ups. Isn't it amazing? When I recounted the number of examples I had given to my son (and which made him run away), I figured that I had touched every aspect of life to explain the concept. This actually reflects how badly we have fallen prey to 'prejudice' in almost everything that we do or deal with. I recalled E. B. White's quote on this topic: "Prejudice is a great time saver. You can form opinions without having to get the facts." While the legendary boxer, Muhammad Ali, had described this as: "Prejudice comes from being in the dark; sunlight disinfects it."

Ponder over it and you will realize that we live in a world full of *prejudice* (ours and theirs) and judge everything through *its* eyes and not ours. Just recall the those instances when you did something, not on your own but under the influence of this 9-letter word, prejudice. Time has come for us to rise above the obvious and take pride in thinking straight from the heart, without giving in to the prejudices that reside deep inside the minds of each one of us.

The insightful conversation with a kid, which caused this chapter, is hereby summed up with the most apt quote—a wonderful quote—by Sir Albert Einstein, one of the greatest persons ever to have lived on earth:

> "*Great spirits have always found violent opposition from mediocrities. The latter cannot understand it when a man does not thoughtlessly submit to hereditary prejudices, but honestly and courageously uses his intelligence.*"
>
> **Albert Einstein**

18 The 13-letter Word

♦

English is a great language. In fact, all languages are wondrous. When you learn a new dialect, there are so many things that you get to learn along with. The best part is, it brings you closer to the culture and traditions associated with that language. For instance, only if you can converse in Japanese (this holds true for all other languages and their corresponding countries), you will be able to understand its people much better. And at the same time you will get to realize how wonderful the country is. But have you ever guessed the magical word which, though remains in the background, but does all the wonders? Well, it is **communication**—the 13-letter word—which resides at the core of anything and everything that we do. Once we know the art of using the underlying theme of this word aptly, we can be ultra-successful in whatever we do—as we are assured of emerging as winners, armed with the skill: 'communication skill.'

But then, we all know that though this magical word is very simple to pronounce, it is very tough to practice and master. I have personally experienced that the root cause of all our problems lies in some form of ineffective communication. It could be a case of under-communication or the reverse—over-communication.

When we close our eyes for a moment and think about all such incidents, which were results of bad communication, we will realize the importance of this word. Let me lead you to some instances, which will help in communicating what is being attempted through this chapter!

How many times have you observed that communication is not flowing smoothly within your organization—either from top to bottom or from bottom to the top (sounds familiar, I presume)? How many times have you shown your frustration with 'the media,' for over-communicating on a petty issue? Do you remember all those communications gaps with your girlfriend/ boyfriend, which resulted in those familiar quarrels? How can you forget all those instances, when people working for you left your organization—simply because your managers could not effectively communicate with them on the issues that troubled them? And what about the communication that flows around with respect to scandals, scams, politics, etc.?

> *So one of the key areas to concentrate, throughout our life is: how we communicate and what we communicate, and a continuous evaluation of the same.*

One of my bosses, with whom I worked in the past, was really passionate about the importance of communication. Being head of a division, he ensured that communication flowed at and through all levels—down to the last and that too, instantly. He used to always tell me, "Communication, not carried out on time, is more or less equivalent to no communication at all. So, either we must communicate instantly or just drop the whole thing. The other benefit of sharing news quickly, whether good or bad, is, it shortens the time that we would spend later—in killing all the rumors, which spread due to delayed communication on your part. Your team(s) must get to know about the ground reality from the 'horse's mouth,' as much as possible, and not rely on unreliable sources of communication, like the conversations that happen at the cafeteria, during smoking sessions and in the corridors."

During one of my routine dinners with him, I asked about the key traits, which he thought were needed in a great communicator. And he replied, "Look, a good communicator is hard to find these days. To me, the one who came closest to being perfect, was Mahatma Gandhi. It was his unique ability to blend good communication skills with his adherence to truth, that gave us the much desired freedom. Gandhi possessed the four distinct qualities of a great communicator: intellectual soundness, emotional maturity, unwavering tolerance and objective orientation." Perfect answer, I must admit.

Yet another perspective to this 13-letter word, is as follows...

Years ago, I was 'attached' to one of the master salesman in my organization. My job was to assist him as a pre-sales solution architect. Within weeks of working with him, I learnt the tricks of how to present the product well and make a killing out of it. One fine day, while we were having lunch, I requested him to enlighten me with some of the best practices that he followed during his successful career. I urged him to share those, until our client—whom we were expecting—arrived. After pondering for few moments, he replied, "Selling is nothing but an art of communicating your thoughts well. You must communicate in a manner, so articulate and crisp, that your customers get the essence of it within the first few minutes itself. Researches have filled reams of pages, time and again, about the normal attention span that we carry as human beings. Therefore, we must utilize it fully...and the only way to do it, is by mastering the art of communicating clearly and succinctly. Of course, I do a lot of homework before meeting my customers, and rehearse my thoughts extremely well around how to start and how to end. And mind you, it has to be perfectly in sync. If you start off well and end up poorly, you are killed. If you start off poorly but end up smartly, then also you get killed. The key to success: *balance your act between the two stages*. What goes on in-between, from start to finish, is what makes the whole difference. On a separate note, do you know how I handle my e-mails?" I replied in the negative.

By now our discussion had gained momentum and he continued enthusiastically... "To be honest with you, I hate e-mails. They are one of the worst forms of communication that I have encountered so far. I do agree that sometimes they work wonders, especially when the distance is quite a bit between the interacting parties, and the time zones have to be countered hence. However, I have never liked the idea of communicating too much through e-mails. There are many reasons to it. First and foremost, e-mails have no emotions. I mean they are devoid of soul. You can't pour your feelings through them. People can perceive your e-mails as rude, while your intentions could be genuine. And again, they can take your e-mails lightly, even when you are shouting: *'Fire! Fire!'* But I don't blame them at all, for perceiving just the reverse. At times, you just can't make out anything from e-mails. So I follow my own rules, which are written on the granite of my consciousness. And I share with you these rules here...

Rule 1: I never write more than two lines, while responding to an e-mail. There are two reasons for the same.

- If I cannot express myself in a crisp and clear manner, through short messages, then I am not articulating them well enough.
- If I have to write more than two lines to explain myself, I pick up the phone instead, and talk.

Rule 2: People around us are very fond of chain-mails these days. You write something and they write back, and then you respond and it goes on and on... My rule around this is again very simple. While still following rule number 1—not writing more than two lines at one go—if my response results in a chain of e-mails, then I simply count the number of times it goes back and forth. The moment it crosses *two levels* in a chain, I drop the ball and set up a face-to-face meeting, even if that means traveling for a day to sort things out. And if it means an overseas travel, then I prefer a video conference and save a few dollars—on travel—for my company.

Adherence to this rule has helped me on innumerable occasions, while dealing with issues that arise out of bad communication. The moment you have a face-to-face meeting, most of it dissolves. The moment you pick up your phone and speak, half of your troubles will end. I have been doing this for years with much resultant success."

He ended the intriguing conversation, paid the check and took me along for the business meeting.

Years have gone by, but I still remember his unwritten rules and have tried to follow them as much as I could (however, I honestly accept that I fail many a times to abide by them).

In keeping with the context of the conversation, I end the chapter with a noble thought shared by one of the **Icelandic educators**:

> *"In a football game—and in the corporate workplace—there is a huge difference between the teams that achieve great success and teams that become dismal failures. The answer is effective communication. Teams that can openly share ideas, focus on the task, and communicate proactively should not be surprised by their achievements."*
>
> **Reed Markham**

19 Follow the Dollar

♥

As I logged-in to my e-mail, I read the corporate announcement about our global president's week-long visit to India. I felt excited in anticipation of meeting him. I had always respected him more than I had anyone else—for his vision, his working style, his leadership, his attention to details. And also, for his love of fancy gadgets and latest software! But unlike some of us, who impulsively buy things and don't use them later, I had always seen him using them in his daily life. It mattered not if he had to spend some time in learning its use. The last time when he came, he carried a model of BlackBerry (which was yet to be launched for people like me), and I simply loved the passion with which he explained its features during one of the corporate dinners. So this time when I came to know of his impending trip, we exchanged e-mails and I asked whether I would see another yet-to-be-released gadget. He replied in just one word, "Surprise!"

For his visit this time, I spent more time than usual on the assignments that I had been working, as there were finer intricacies involved. During one of the inter-city travels to another offshore center of ours in India, we spent good time on the plane together. I asked about a few of his favorite things, his focus for the next few years and how he managed everything so well for a multi-billion dollar enterprise that we were working for. As our conversation progressed, he gave me a wonderful piece of advice: "One of the things that my father taught me very early in my life was to respect the dollar. He always told me: *'If you wish to be successful in managing your own expenses, just follow the dollar.'"*

He continued... "So whenever I struggle with my own finances—or with the finances of our business units—I simply take the time to deeply analyze how the dollar travels within our BU (business unit), and how it is being spent. Once I am through with this exercise, I know how it affects the top line and bottom line for us. In the process, if I need to make changes, I do so before it is too late to react. No matter how good a strategist and visionary you are, if you don't know how to follow the dollar, and track expenses vis-à-vis profits, you would always fall flat. Do this exercise yourself. If you keep track of all expenses and follow the dollar diligently, you will invent newer and better ways to manage your finances. And if you can manage your finances well, you can keep most of the troubles away."

This conversation instantly reminded me of Mahatma Gandhi's similar views on the importance of tracking expenses, which I had read in his autobiography. During his stay in London, since he used to get money from his brother, he kept a track of his money meticulously. He acknowledged this as one of the good habits he had picked during his tenure in London, and thus urged: "Let every youth take a leaf out of my book and make it a point to account for everything that comes into, and goes out of, his pocket. And like me, he is sure to be a gainer in the end."

And what the global president told me that day could be also stated as: *if we are able to track our expenses well, we will be able to derive more from what we are earning. This will result in creating lesser dissatisfaction with our jobs—something, which I see happening very frequently with the young kids in the IT industry these days.*

A Chinese proverb describes this advice so beautifully: "Money well-spent is money well-used."

So, get a sticker at your workplace which always reminds you of this simple, yet so powerful, principle: "Follow the dollar!"

P.S. He did share the 'surprise,' the moment he landed in India! He had switched from a BlackBerry to an Android smartphone from Samsung (yet again, before its worldwide release☺).

20 Don't be a Bozo

♠

If you have read about Steve Jobs and his eccentricity, then you will know where this chapter is leading to—because bozo is a term patented by Steve. ☺. Steve being one of my favorite icons, I have read about him extensively. In of the books by Jay Elliot, on Steve, this term has been explained beautifully. Steve had always believed in hiring the best talents: astonishing brains, with 'three-digit, 110+ IQ scores.' Anyone with a lesser score would automatically fall under the 'bozo' category. Of course, other reasons were mentioned too, which would immediately transfer anyone into that category. But for the purpose of this chapter, we will consider only the parameter of IQ scores.

Over the years, I too have learnt that if we want to *produce* the best-in-class, we need to *hire* the *breed* which is the best-in-class. More often than not, we just concentrate on matching the job skills while hiring and thus, lose focus on parameters like IQ, EQ, etc. The repercussions of such decisions are very much apparent in the long-term—and in certain cases, even prove to be very costly.

Here is a rule of thumb to calculate quick damages: *higher is the extent of hiring, greater the damages would be for making a mistake.* You can still afford to take chances, while hiring junior-level staff. But what would happen, if tomorrow you need to cross-train such people for something else (market behaves that way all the time)? If you have hired the wrong set of people, you are dead. If you hired them wrong, you end up hiring more of them—because tomorrow, they are ones who will be hiring for you. And before you realize, the whole city (read: the organization) would get infected, just like the way Umbrella Corp did, in the *Resident Evil* series.

On the contrary, we always do the opposite. We hire campus graduates mostly on the basis of their high IQ and aptitude scores. On the other hand, we give preference to experience and matching set of skills *only* for hiring senior and middle level staff. I am not saying that skills and experience do not count. In fact, they do very much. However, my observation is with respect to the higher preference given to these parameters, only when we move up in the hierarchy. Most of the times, when I sit with my hiring team to review the reasons behind rejecting candidates, I have noticed IQ scores figuring last—in the list of criteria for eligibility. Most of the members on the hiring panel, from the 'service delivery' side, seem to give more weightage to parameters like technical skills, experience, etc. In some cases, I find that rejection is made on petty grounds, such as not having CICS (customer information control system) knowledge, while working on mainframes for years. In my opinion, CICS is something which can be learned quickly, if the person concerned has a good aptitude and shows willingness to learn and adapt.

Once, a famous CEO was questioned on how he chooses his team and he replied, "I choose my team based on my *weaknesses*, so that 'they' can fill-in for *them* and convert *them* into my *strengths*. It is like strategizing in the battlefield. If you are weak on one side of the fortress that you have built, you better put your best fighters to defend you on those spots. You can't fight, defending all sides of the fortress, even if you are invincible and immortal. Similarly, each one of us, no matter how smart we are, has a set of weaknesses. So when I need to hire and build a team, I ensure that I cover my weaknesses well by hiring the right set of people." Brilliant observation, indeed.

So the next time you need to hire people for your team, don't be a bozo. Because if you act like a bozo, you will end up recruiting more of them and thus, would be creating a 'bozo world' around yourself. Hire the right people with good IQ, even if the skills on the job do not match perfectly. If they are not bozos, it will just be a matter of time before they pick up the required skills and become an asset for you.

Here is what one of the leading players said when he was questioned—about the strategy he had adopted—after winning a gold medal in the Olympics:

> ***"If you are a player and you aim for winning a gold medal for yourself, you better get trained by ex-gold medal winners."***

21 Secret of the Dragon Scroll

♣

One of my all-time favorite movies is the hilarious and cute, and at the same time very inspirational, *Kungu Fu Panda Part 1*. To start with, I love its tagline: "Prepare for awesomeness."

For those who have not yet seen this brilliantly crafted movie, the story and its backdrop, in brief, follows...

The story is set in the 'Valley of Peace': a fictional land in ancient China, inhabited by anthropomorphic animals. Po, a clumsy panda, is a kung fu fanatic, who idolizes the furious five: tigress, monkey, mantis, viper and crane—a team of kung fu masters, trained by the red panda, master Shifu, to protect the valley. Because he works at his goose father, Mr. Ping's noodle restaurant, Po is unable to achieve his dream of becoming a kung fu master. One day, Shifu's mentor, the old tortoise, master Oogway, has a vision that Shifu's former student and adopted son, the evil snow leopard, Tai Lung, will escape from prison and return to the 'Valley of Peace' to take revenge—for being denied the dragon scroll, which is said to hold the secret to limitless power.

When master Shifu hands over the dragon scroll to Po and asks him to open—and read—it, Po finds that the scroll has nothing written inside. The only thing that he could see, was his own reflection. Everyone, including master Shifu, is baffled to find that the dragon scroll is blank. All these years, they had believed master Oogway, who had been repeatedly saying that only 'the chosen one' will be able to read the secret of the dragon scroll and thus, become 'the dragon warrior.'

Subsequent to this, at the behest of master Shifu the villagers flee from the village…and hence from Tai Lung's terror. During that time, Po's father, Mr. Ping, reveals a secret of his delicious noodles in order to pass that legacy to his son, Po.

Herein, I share the profound beauty of their conversation...

Mr. Ping: "The secret ingredient is...nothing!"

Po: "Huh?"

Mr. Ping: "You heard me. Nothing! There is no secret ingredient."

Po: "Wait, wait...it is just a plain old noodle soup? You don't add some kind of special sauce or something?"

Mr. Ping: "Don't have to. To make something special, you just have to *believe* it is special."

[Po looks at the scroll again, and sees his reflection in it.]

Po[speaks to himself]: "There is no secret ingredient..."

And then Po realizes the *secret, hidden message* inside the dragon scroll: *believing in self and believing that one can do it* (whatever be the endeavor).

Po ultimately defeats Tai Lung using the secret 'Wuxi Finger Hold.'

One learning that I have always told my son to take from this movie is to believe in himself…always. In fact, I call this phenomenon as 'self-discovery.' Often, there lies so much within us, hidden like a treasure. Just like we played treasure hunt as kids, life too presents clues to us—to unlock that hidden potential, and perform at a level that only winners can achieve.

All we need is self-belief. It keeps reminding us of our true potential, and pats us on our back when we achieve the seemingly unattainable. There had been many such incidents in my life wherein, at the onset, I felt as if I was the most incompetent person for that task. However, once I wired my brain to believe that I was 'the' person to accomplish the task—the best one—I not only accomplished it, but also emerged as a winner.

Instances of teenagers getting attracted towards drugs—simply because deep inside they suffer from low self-esteem and thus are low on self-confidence—stare at us menacingly. While we blame the teenagers for taking this route, we often fail to attribute it to their upbringing and surroundings. Unknowingly, as parents, teachers, friends and elders, we end up drawing unnecessary comparisons with their peers—and thereby, damage their tender and highly impressionable minds more than we could ever imagine.

Jack Trout has always maintained: ***"Battles are fought in the mind and not on the ground,"*** and I completely agree with his observation.

And **Dan Hawkins**, the former head coach of the University of Colorado Buffaloes, said it so well:

> ***"Hey, if its only about winning, count me out. Its about the approach you take—not just in football but also in life. You should be willing to take risks and above all, to believe in yourself."***

22 Instant Redemption

♦

Unlike coffee, there are a few things which taste best when served instantly: instant redemption of reward points, instant noodles, instant cash backs, instant discount coupons...and yes, instant appreciation!

Let us talk about the last one, but definitely not the least, in the list. Shall we? Close your eyes and think: when was the last time that you wrote a note of appreciation to someone who does not work directly for you? The term 'directly,' is being used for those who are in our team either as a supervisor or as a junior or as a contemporary. We say thanks to such people with whom we work directly; but what about those with whom the association is indirect?

I am sure you can envisage what I am trying to convey here. Most of us, find the routine eight hours of work in a day to be too short to complete our never ending list of tasks. Thus, we all crave to work at a pace fast enough to fit-in everything that we can in the available timeframe. In doing so, we come across many people who help us achieve our day-to-day objectives, and help us to gain and enjoy the 'tag' of super-efficient. My 'admin' staff, my mail room assistant, my HR guy, my finance manager—the list would be endless if I start counting such people.

We come across so many people who come ahead and enable us to do our jobs better and faster. Yet, we fail to appreciate them—most of the times. Sometimes, even when we do it, it is done as the last thing on our 'to do' list—taken up with a 'when time permits' kind of approach. We create a 'to do' list every day and put this 'thanksgiving' in there, at the last. We assume that one day, if our boss is really pleased with us, we might get a chance to reach the last item on our 'to do' list and thus, will be able to write that 'thank you' note we always dream of writing. In reality, we must do the opposite: strike out that last item in the list and place it at the top, preceding even the 'number 1' on that list. Come on, be honest! How much time does it take to write two or three lines of good words about and to the person who helped you meet your everyday deadlines? If we are good at 'text-ing' messages or e-mails, it won't take more than 60 seconds of our schedule. *I bet we can easily steal those 'rare' 60 seconds from our schedule, and write one "Thank you" note daily.*

Trust me... Just like the other instant wonders that I have mentioned at the beginning of the chapter, this act of ours is going to give us the same level of gratification that we derived while earning those double reward points on our last purchase at the supermarket—*and add to it, the immeasurable innate satisfaction.* Sometimes, small acts like the "Thank you" notes, go a long way in ensuring healthy bonding—be it in our professional or personal lives.

I still remember a person, who was really good at this. He once told me...

"These e-mails and text messages are actually meant for reducing distances. But in reality, they have increased the distances between us in multiples. We have become dependent on technology more, than on anything else. We now prefer to send e-mails—or text messages—even to the person sitting at the adjacent cabin, rather than walking up to him/her. I have made a golden rule that I follow as much as I can. The rule may sound primitive: I always go to the person and appreciate him/her by saying thanks, in person. I shake hands and acknowledge how thankful I am for the helping gesture shown by the person. Sometimes, I even give a handwritten card. And again, at times, I also tell my fellow colleagues to just stand up and have a round of applause for the great work that person has done for me. The personal touch seems to be moving away from us and we must do everything to bring it back in our lives."

Very well said!

Let us take a look at some of the reciprocations, that my "Thank you" gestures have received:

- "You made my day!"
- "I have been working here for so many years. Yet no one ever thought of thanking me. I know my work is far less important than yours, but still, your 'thank you' note made me feel very important."
- "I never thought that you would come to my seat and say thanks to me for the work that I did. You took me by huge surprise."
- "I have realized today, how happy one can feel by getting a one-line *'Thank you'* note. You know why? Because I felt the same today—and only because of you. So, thank you!"
- "I could not have expected anything better than this on a Friday morning!"
- "Before I received this handwritten card, I used to feel that SMSs are the best way to convey our feelings. I was wrong. A card can say a thousand words more, filled with emotions. Your words energized me."
- "I am feeling as if I am very important for the company. Thank you for making me feel so special."
- "Frankly, I had never thought of thanking people who work for me. I always used to think: *'So what? It is their job to help me out.'* But when I got the e-mail from you and read its content, I realized how a small gesture can fill your day with all the happiness."

So please place on the top of your 'to do' list…starting today: *"Let your coffee be brewed and your appreciations be instant."* ☺.

23 Getting on Your Soapbox? Watch Out!

♥

Life is full of contradictions. People claim that they want health- food, but our very own McDonalds still makes billions of dollars each year. People affirm: they want to work for companies that provide job satisfaction, yet end up doing just the reverse—chasing the one offering the biggest paycheck. They state that they want to watch news on world affairs, but tune-in to 24×7 coverage of 'MTV Grind.' ☺

There is no harm in being a *little* contradictory and do as one wishes. However, when it comes to advising others on what to do and what to avoid, we must be extra-careful. *Getting on your soapbox is easy, but being true to what you are preaching is something which is not that easy.*

Almost every day, I get calls from—or meet—people who are out to sell something. They try to sell their products to me, as an individual or to my organization, by pitching-in with their salient features. 'Need' is a very important factor for me when I go to buy something. At the same time, I filter out genuine people by carrying a simple test called 'the moment of truth.' (The name of a famous television series inspires the name of this test; but my test is not as tough as participating in that series was!)

For the test, all I do is ask a few simple questions, answers to which immediately prove whether the company, or the person in question, is really serious about what they (he) preach(es).

Let me give you a couple of examples. There was an executive who once tried to sell a particular bank's credit card to me. He went on to explain all the features of the card, and also assured that it would earn four times the reward points at select outlets. I kept on listening. After he was through, I decided to play my very own, 'the moment of truth,' game. I started (round 1, question 1): "Do you use credit cards?" He said, "Yes." I continued (round 1, question 2)... "May I see your credit card, since I am sure the great credit card that you are trying to sell would be your preferred one?" There you go. He carried a card of some other bank. He failed in round 1 itself.

Then there was another instance. A sales person of a reputed cellular phone company tried to sell me a new plan they had come out with. As usual, the agent did a great job, explaining all that I would get: free talk-time, free messages every month, great network coverage and an unlimited data plan. Once he was through, he could not have even imagined what was coming next: my very own game.

Question 1: "Since I may need some time to think about this great plan, can I come back to you?"

Answer: "Yes."

Question 2: "May I have your contact number?"

Answer: "Sure. Here it is."

And he gave me the cell number, of the phone provided by his company. I thought he was about to pass and just then, his personal cell phone rang.

Question 3: "You have a fancy personal cell phone. What plan do you have on this one?"

Answer: Gotcha! That was it! He said that he used a competitor's services ...beep... Another one failed the test.

A few days later, I met some of the executives of a company which dealt with 'mobility solutions.' With them, I had an altogether different experience. These guys impressed me.

As they began their presentation, using an iPad for the purpose, it was absolutely clear that they were truly mobile. They did not carry any laptops and had only iPads. While I was happy to see their approach, I still *had* to play the game with them. Round 1, question 1: "Suppose you are on the road, and with no access to your 'PC.' In that case, how do you fill your timesheet?" One of their executives stood up and opened an application on his iPad to show that he could still fill his timesheet using his mobile device. Bravo! Round 1 cleared. Round 2, question 1: "How do you fill your expense report?" He opened another application on his iPad, and showed how he used it to complete his expense reports. And do you know what was the best part? He used an 'application' (software), which was developed by his own company. After two more rounds, I was very happy to see that these executives represented a truly mobile company and 'walked the talk.' They had full confidence in the solutions they were selling—simply because they believed in their own solutions. They passed the 'the moment of truth' test successfully. End result: I recommended them to my clients immediately.

So next time, whichever side of the game you are on, just play it with honesty. I am sure, you will be outstanding as you stand on the soapbox.

24 Choose Your Own Race!

♠

During my graduation two good things happened to me: I met the girl of my dreams, and I met one of the best teachers in my life—an incident which I cherish much. He not only taught me fundamentals of engineering, but also the fundamentals of life. Being very close to me, he spent good deal of time, explaining the nuances of life and how they must be treated with respect. After hitting the gym every evening, I used to spend time—on alternate evenings—with my girlfriend and my teacher.

In one of our countless coffee sessions, which normally used to last for 30-40 minutes, we discussed racing. On that particular day, he was in an exceptionally good mood and that ensured some good "Life lessons" from him that day.

Enjoying his coffee, he began...

"Most of the time, you will see kids about your age running the same race and trying very hard to win it. It is the same, while you are in school. It then gets carried over to your days in university—and then finally, it is all over the place in the corporate world. You compete not to learn, but to win. Also, while running those mindless marathons, you forget pondering over one basic question: *'Is your body fit for marathons, or is it built for the 100m or the 200m dash, or is it designed for the relays?'* Not everyone can win marathons. But if they choose their own race, they will surely win."

The conversation which had started like the light evening

breeze, became as flavored as the coffee we were sipping. In fact, I began enjoying it more and more and hence, asked, "You mean, we must choose our own race?"

He replied, "Yes. That is what we all must strive for. Running your own race carries multiple connotations. One of them could be: follow your heart and do what it says, rather than blindly following the herd. You need to enjoy the journey—rather than worrying about the destination—though it is good to keep an eye on the destination. The real happiness is derived from the journey you undertake to reach there. I have seen many kids, burning the midnight oil during their undergraduate years, and then carry it forward to their corporate lives—only to realize later that they chose the wrong race. And even if they look like winners, in reality they are the biggest losers. Because they chose the wrong race. And most of the times, it is too late to go back and start a new one, since your biological clock just calls it a day."

He continued... "When I was a kid, one of my gurus taught me: *'If you follow the crowd, the place you will most likely end up is the exit'.*"

I agreed and asked, "And what is the other reason for running a race of our own?"

He took a long sip, before replying, "Creativity is missing in kids these days. They follow the conventional. They don't reason things. Maybe, parenting has a lot to do with it. Parents, these days, do not have the time to answer all the questions that invade and reside in an adolescent's mind. Over the years, such kids fine-tune themselves to the conventional approaches, which are safer and do not require a lot of reasoning. The reason behind this is the lack of encouragement—and support—that parents should be extending to their kids when they are growing up with multitude of questions in their mind. When their questions are smothered repeatedly, their creativity is choked. They develop an inhibitive approach towards life, and thus prefer the comfort of convention.

No wonder, the kids working in laboratories and workshops mostly follow the instructions. *They do not question. And when you don't question, you become conventional.* You start doing *only* what others tell you to do, and in the process, you lose the ability to think differently and unconventionally. These kids are extremely good in theory. But when it comes to the practical (the application of the theory that they have learnt), they are found woefully wanting. You know what? When I evaluate kids like you during a practical exam, I measure you on what I call: a 'maverick-o-meter scale.' This scale rates you on how differently you can think. I really don't mind if your experiments do not give you the expected results, as long as you know what you are doing—and more importantly, why you are doing it. I rate such people high on the 'maverick-o-meter' scale. To me, they are the ones who would do well in life, and by now, you know what is *my definition* of *'doing well.' It is not about how high you reach. It is all about enjoying the journey to the destination—even if the pinnacle is not as high as others might have reached.*"

We both laughed and bade each other goodbye for the day.

Years have passed by, but I still see most of the folks running what I now term a 'rented race,' and not their own. The new kids—the fresh ones—who join me right after their graduation, run a race for MBA or MS, not realizing: whether they are really made for it; whether this is what their heart truly wants; and whether such a thing is going to give them the happiness and satisfaction that they yearn for. In addition to this, I see some of them leaving their bright IT careers midway to become a manager with some MNC bank, selling savings accounts. ☺. Best of luck to all of them!

However, I wonder if this was what they *really* wanted to do all these years. I don't think they followed what their heart wanted. In fact, I feel they never spent any time on thinking what they wanted to be in reality. Over time, they lost their ability to stop for a while, take rest and think about the goals which would lead them to real happiness. On the contrary, they seemed to be simply interested in running that race which offered the highest prize money and thus, boast of being the highest paid among their Facebook friends. Thanks to the gentleman who coined the term 'peer pressure.' It saves millions on this planet, as they use it as an excuse for running a race which is not really their own.

If one really wants to understand the concept behind running one's own race, I would suggest one dives deep into Steve Jobs' life and learn how he chose his own races and emerged as a winner. During all these years, I feel so blessed using Apple's products—not because of Steve's personality, but because Apple really 'thinks differently.' He and his team members would have surely scored a perfect 10 on my teacher's 'maverick-o-meter' scale. And this is what I too strive for all the time. When I get into situations where I have to choose between options, I make the choice which may appear difficult to implement. It rates me very high on my teacher's scale, and brings me closer to Steve's working style!

While reading **Michael Porter**, I came across an elegant explanation:

> ***"Operational effectiveness means you are running the same race, but faster. But strategy is choosing to run a different race—because it is the one you have set yourself up to win."***

Brilliant perspective, I must acknowledge.

And the very context of the chapter brings me to conclude it with a befitting line from one of my favorite movies, ***Kung Fu Panda Part 2:***

> ***"One often meets his destiny on the road he takes to avoid it."***
>
> Master Oogway

25 Being Human!

While reading a book on Mother Teresa, I came across a wonderful thought of hers: "In this life we cannot always do great things, but we can do small things with great love." *Simply beautiful declaration from a being devoted to God and humanity.*

One of the best things that corporates practice nowadays is what we typically refer to as 'corporate social responsibility' (CSR). Almost all the companies that I have worked for, had some kind of CSR cell or department. To me, it is a wonderful way of giving back something to the society. More than your hard earned money, the society needs your time and your presence to help the underprivileged and the old.

This chapter requires a special mention of one of my friends, as she has given an altogether new meaning to the concept behind CSR. The best thing that I like about her is the passion she brings on the table while heading the CSR-cell, apart from her official responsibilities. I have seen her spending long hours at the old age homes, blind schools and the orphanages. She would celebrate birthdays of her team members in such places, and instill the joy of giving to anyone and everyone she met. She is always at the helm of blood donation camps and old clothes collection drives. Not everyone has the guts to sacrifice the weekends for such services. But I can proudly say that she has.

Whenever we meet our clients from different countries, she would passionately talk about how her CSR team had been actively *giving back* to the society. She would hand over printed booklets and brochures, to publicize the NGOs that our company is associated with. No wonder, many of our clients donate large sums to such institutions for whom she works.

She once observed: "The days of corporate social responsibility are over. We must now switch over to personal social responsibility. Then only we will be able to bring the much needed reforms in the society. It is tough, but someone needs to make that very first move, and that *I will*." I still remember her favorite quip: "Life is an echo. What you send out, you get back. What you give, you get."

You feel so satisfied and complete, once you have donated something—whether it is your own blood, your clothes or your money. More important, than what is being donated, is the mindset—the intention—behind it. One of the things that I have personally experienced within, is peace.

I often make my donations through my 11-year old son. And there is a valid reason behind this act of mine. I want him to get into this habit of parting away with his favorite things and that too, happily. I know, he is too young to get into the art of giving. But again, unless he gets into the groove now, it will be difficult for him to get into it later. *So, sooner it is, the better.* I remember one such instance, when we participated in a toy collection drive in our housing society. I had convinced my son to part away with some of his favorite toys, which I made him donate to the underprivileged kids—with his very own hands. (Between us, I ensured that he got a new set of toys a few days after the drive!) He needs to understand, and feel, the pain the underprivileged kids go through every day and thus, has to be thankful to God for whatever has been bestowed upon him.

As a rule of thumb, we now keep a bag—full of old clothes—in the dickey of our cars. One never knows where we would come across such needy people who could be benefited by them.

Another friend of mine correlated the intentions (or otherwise) to serve the society with that individual's SQ (spiritual quotient). He once told, "You need to inspire the folks around you to find an objective in their life, and there can be nothing more pleasing than helping those who need the most."

Thus, anyone who joins my business unit (BU) gets to meet me within a few days of joining. I meet them individually or in a group. Apart from letting them know about the vision, and the guiding principles of my BU, I normally end such meetings by urging them to give back to the society, whenever life gives them an opportunity to do so.

A friend of mine shared his perspective in this context... "Here is the deal: when we spend time with the underprivileged, it often helps in changing our perspective and thus, leads us to look at things differently. There was a time when our teenage sons started treating us badly. They used to shout back even at the slightest of remarks made by any one of us, and simply would not listen to us. So on the birthday of one of the sons, we took them to an orphanage. I made them spend the entire day with orphan kids, cutting across all age groups, and made them prepare lunch with these kids. I made them donate clothes too. And you know what? That very day they realized, how their world would be without their parents around. I could see *that* respect in their eyes, *which* had been missing for years. They realized our value, and appreciated the sacrifices parents often make for the happiness of their kids."

He recalled further...

> "Similarly, there was a time when my younger son was too much into electronic gadgets, and would often spend hours in front of LCD panels of all sorts. Despite our best efforts to control his usage of the same, he just would not listen. So now you can guess, where I took him. Yes! I took him to a blind school and made him spend time with those kids. I still remember that after coming back he spent a good amount of time in front of the mirror, touching his own eyes, having thus realized how important they were to his life. He started taking care of his eyes from that day itself."

People often term social service as a rich man's way of

spending time and money. I often come across many people, who sarcastically comment behind the back of such 'donors': "He has money, and that is why he is donating it." Well, I do understand the difference between a person earning 2 grand a month and donating 100$ to a cause, compared to a person earning 10 grand a month and donating the same amount to a cause. However, I still beg to differ. We have to acknowledge the fact that despite having money, the person still has to have the guts to part with it. There are still many of us out there, earning millions, yet not giving away even a cent to the society. And then there is another aspect pertaining to donations. Instead of explaining it, I choose to share an incident in brief with you—as that would hit the nail on its head. The owner of a large business house was once seen donating a huge sum of money to a blind school. When confronted by a reporter on why he was donating such a large sum, he answered, "It may look worthless to you, but not to those who have a blind child at home."

In this context I am reminded of a quote that I read years ago, but I still feel rejuvenated whenever I read it. Hence, the same is being shared with you all:

> ***"The best thing about giving away is, what we get is always better than what we give. The reaction is greater than the action."***
>
> **Orison Swett Marden**

P.S. This is the right chapter to mention something about the "Being Human Foundation."

I, as the author of this book, take pride in my association with the "Being Human Foundation."

The "Salman Khan Foundation" works in the areas of education and healthcare for the underprivileged in India. Salman Khan believes that there is still a lot to be done in both the areas. The work done by the "Being Human Foundation" is closest to his heart.

Know more about "Being Human Foundation" at:

http://beinghumanonline.com.

26 Nothing Stays Forever!

♦

As I was driving back from office after a day's work, my cell phone rang. I was delighted to hear the voice on the other end as I answered the call. Even though it had been years, I recognized her voice instantly. She was an ex-colleague of mine; we used to work together years ago. One of the reasons for recognizing her voice instantly was the fact that her memories were still very fresh in my mind. She was one of the very few people that I had admired and cherished working with, during the early years of my professional career. Now that we were with different companies, I missed her even more... And this had kept the memories alive.

She was better than me in almost all domains of work. Yet she was very humble about her competence, and never used it to gain brownie points. I clearly remember how she had helped me on a number of occasions: pulling me out of difficult situations with the programming, and helping me debug the mess out of it. She would do it as if it was her own assignment and that is what differentiated her from the rest. We became good friends, but soon I switched over to a new company. After few weeks, she too switched over to a new job and went abroad. Slowly, we lost touch, even though we chatted once in a while on LinkedIn.

So, after refreshing the memory , I asked about her whereabouts. She told me that she was now back in India, and for good. I was delighted by the news. We decided to meet over lunch one day and celebrate our good old days. After struggling with our schedules for few days, we finally met. The very first reaction, when I met her, was not a good one. She had changed completely. No more the vivacious and cheerful person I knew, she came across as a very serious person. She spoke little, and was 'to the point' with her replies and queries. In fact, it felt as if we were both participating in a Q&A session, where both of us answered the questions being asked.

After the initial few minutes of our conversation, I could not control myself anymore and asked if everything was well with her. I took the initiative, stating gently, "Look here, I know something is not well and I can see that written all over your face. It is perfectly fine if you do not want to share it with me. But if you share, I assure you of two things: it will lighten your heart; and I could do my bit, and see if I can help."

After a pause, she opened up and continued for long, while I listened. She spoke about how her life had turned upside-down by choosing the wrong person as her life partner; how she had to handle an abusive husband, despite the fact that they had married after working together for many months in the States; how she managed the emotional breakdown, in an alien country, with neither relatives nor parents; how she contemplated ending her life, when she felt it was too much to bear this burden anymore; and finally, calling it quits with her husband, to return to her motherland. As she spoke, I could see her eyes welling up, with tears trying hard *not* to roll down her cheeks. But I pretended not to notice them. I wanted her to feel brave and confident, and not like a loser.

As she paused, I began...

> "You know what? Let me first congratulate you for being so brave to walk out of a relationship that has brought more sorrows than happiness. We live with relations so that we can derive happiness out of them. The moment such relations start hitting us back, and hard, we must be brave enough to walk away from them. I am so happy to see that you already have taken that first step."

I had already ordered some coffee and sandwiches to munch on, because I knew this was going to be a *long* conversation. Here I was, sitting with a longtime friend, who badly needed good advice from her buddy. These are the times when we need a friend who can sit with us, listen and then show us the right path.

I continued... "Now, there is something that we all need to keep at the back of our minds: *nothing stays forever*. This is one rule, which has been chiseled in granite with carvings of gold. Whether it is your good days or the bad ones, they eventually leave you and go away. So, if you are too much into celebrating your good days, or sulking over your bad ones, both are equally injurious to your emotional well-being and hence, they must be avoided at all times. There will be times in your life when the good days leave you in a blink of an eye, while the bad ones choose to stay longer than you had expected—and vice-versa. However, the rule is ever valid: *everything is temporary and will finally go away one day*."

She kept listening and I could see that she was feeling far better than she had been, when we started. I concluded with: "Never forget that you can still see stars, even in the darkest of hours—provided you want to see them, and believe that there are many more out there. The hope and belief, together, will always make you derive newer meaning from your life, even if the previous meaning failed to prove its worth. Now that you are back, take charge of your life and start living it fully."

In order to lighten her mood, I made her remember how I used to make stupid 'coding' mistakes, and how she, being the intelligent one, would spot them by just glancing at the code—that too with just one eye open! I told her that again the time had come when she must once recognize her true worth—and yet again, see life with just one eye open...just the way she did before.

I promised to keep in touch to ensure that she stays focused and firm, en route to getting her life back on track. After many weeks, she got married again. This time, everything went well. As I write this chapter, remembering her, she has a beautiful daughter, three years old, who keeps her ultra-busy. And yes, she has started treating herself and her life very well once again—*and with just one eye open*. ☺.

27 Don't be a Black Hole

♥

As kids, we used to be highly fascinated by the theory behind black holes. Or should I say stories of black holes enamored us, since our teachers explained black holes in such a simple manner? Their explanation was: "If something goes into a black hole, it will never come back...not even light." And thus, I used to visualize black holes as gates to some kind of magical portal where, if you entered once, the doors would close by themselves—transporting you to a different 'realm' for the rest of your life. Little did I realize that when I grow up, I would experience so many of them in the corporate world that the abstruseness around them would no longer remain a magical mystery, but would turn into a harsh reality.

Picture this for a minute: how many times have you observed that you e-mailed a question to someone within your organization, and nothing came back in return? Sounds familiar? You then assumed that the person might be busy or traveling. So you waited for some more time, then sent a reminder, hoping that at least *this time* you would get something in return. And you waited and waited and waited...

Did you forget that when something goes into a black hole, it never returns?

Since I have spent significant amount of time, researching

upon these corporate black holes, I decided to come out with my own hypothesis around their behavior, types, characteristics, etc.—though I am yet to file a patent for the same. ☺.

Let us discuss their types first. There are two types of black holes in the corporate universe. The primary characteristics of the first type, and because of which you can easily identify them, are their exceptional abilities to remain politically correct all the time. They want to please everyone around. Hence, they follow firmly their belief: 'no decision' is the best decision, under any and all circumstances. So in reality, this type consists of people who are poor decision-makers. Again, there are two tribes within this group: people who *do not want* to take a decision (let us name them as CAT 1A), and people who *do not know* how to take a decision (likewise named, CAT 1B).

CAT 1A is the most common, of all the species of black holes moving around us. You will find them almost everywhere. They will frustrate you to death, but will not respond. Because if they respond, they will have to take a decision and if they take a decision, they will have to be on one side of the road. I have come across a lot of them. *They are easy to recognize and hard to tolerate!* Here are some examples. Suppose, you are in the middle of a task and you want them to take a decision, which they choose not to. Bingo! You have found your first corporate black hole. The decision will go into an ever-pending state. And again, there are instances when you are close to make a sale and the person you were dealing with unmasks himself (typical of the last few minutes of a Hitchcock movie), to reveal his true identity: a black hole.

CAT 1B, on the other hand, will add some fun to your life. While they are equally frustrating to deal with, they would still give you an opportunity to have a laugh over a mug of beer on a Friday afternoon. Just close your eyes and recall their action (or reaction) and you will surely end up with a smile on your face. This type will never realize the fact that they cannot take a decision—*not that they don't want to; they are not just able to.* They are highly incompetent, and they do not even know about it. So, all you end up doing is, bang your head against the walls of their offices, trying to explain the inexplicable (to them)—'the logic.' You get into a meeting, hoping that a decision would be made. But you come out of the same meeting, with *another date*, for *another meeting*. (Who says sequels don't work? They are hugely popular in corporate boardrooms!) And sometimes, all this is executed with such charm and élan that it makes *you* feel as if you are the one who is on the wrong side of the law, trying to complicate matters of professional interest. ☺.

Let us now come to the characteristics of the second category. *They are the ones who do not really care about who you are.* They carry this firm belief that people like us belong to an alien planet, and aliens should never be considered as friends. Hence, anything coming from aliens should be killed almost instantly. Thus, they simply shoot everything down by hitting the delete button, as soon as they get your e-mail or voicemail. *Their prominent characteristics are their rudeness and arrogance.* They believe that they have all the power in this universe, and it is to be used to rule the world (oppressing the world, would be a better description of their intent). They will look at us as mere pawns laid on a chessboard, where they consider themselves to be the undisputed kings. (Who would go and educate them that one can still checkmate them using pawns?)

A variant of this species is slightly more intelligent, given that they are not really rude. They pretend to be extremely busy all the time—as if the country's economy lies in their hands, and they have been entrusted with the special responsibility to save the world from another recession. So, if you bump into one of them and ask about the e-mail that you had sent, they will come up, much too sweetly, with many sugar-coated quips: "Oh! Is it? Did you send that to me? When did you send it? I don't think I have received it yet (as if e-mails would stop in-between, have a pint of beer somewhere en route, before reaching his BlackBerry). I tell you, these assistants are good for nothing. She did not tell me anything about it." But the truth still remains the same. Such people really do not care about who you are.

Contrary to the groups and sub-groups discussed above, I remember meeting a C-level executive, during one of my trips to Japan, who had stated, "One of the things I ensure is that I read all the e-mails that come to me. It really does not matter whether I am in the 'To' or the 'Cc'/'Bcc' column. I do glance at them too, to make sure that I am not missing something genuine. Sometimes, your employees approach you using this medium, because they feel safe. Since they don't have to face you, they feel comfortable writing their heart out. And if you miss out on such e-mails, then you are probably distancing yourself from your employees. Each day, I keep aside 60 minutes of my day to go through e-mails which pour into my mailbox from faraway places. I never get to finish them during those 60 minutes, but I carry them forward to the next day. The crux is: they never get deleted or archived, unless I have seen them or acted upon them." He remains one of my best idols around, and is highly engaged with his employee base—a true opposite to the corporate black holes.

Therefore, the next time you see an e-mail which is seeking some response, and is not from your boss, do not add yourself to the ever growing population of the corporate black holes. Show that e-mail light of the day with your response, and be different in the process.

28 Do Yourself a Favor...Meet Them

♠

I consider myself lucky enough, having spent time with some great people in my life, whereby, I also got the opportunity to learn from their experiences. In fact, I picked this habit—which I am about to mention—from one of my earlier bosses. He used to often advise, "We must never leave even an iota of a chance to meet great people, even if that means: picking/dropping them from/to the airport, or snatching those rare few minutes over high tea or at the corporate dinner events, and many such occasions that come."

Time and again, I have often pondered over its perceived value and mused: *is it true that meeting great people, even if for a few minutes, is immensely beneficial?* After careful observation, I am led to the response: *yes...the benefits are immense.* Indeed, such interactions have always resulted in enhancing my learning, and of course, learning in real time. A few minutes spent with the people whom you admire is hundred times more productive than 'reading them' through books/magazines. Though, their own views, written either by them or in print—verbatim (interviews)—are highly beneficial, as they come from the horse's mouth. It is for the same reason that I have always loved reading quotes by great people. They have this unique ability to convey a lot more, despite expressing in few words. I have many such 'apps,' downloaded into everything that I use (tablet, smartphone, etc.). And the first minute that I get free (could be while waiting for a doctor's appointment or at the airport…the location could be any), I use these 'apps' to read quotes to keep myself inspired all the time.

As regards meeting people of eminence, I am not saying that greatness lies only within the 'Forbes' world. Not at all. It could be anyone. It could be someone at your office, whom you have heard being spoken very highly of; it could be one of your friend's friend who has been very successful in his career; it could be one of your favorite authors; it could be one of those celebrities that you have always admired; it could be one of those people whose quotes you have been reading all these years or it could even be one of the teachers, because of whom, you are what you are today.

No matter how time consuming or hard it may sound, we must always go ahead and meet such people, whenever life gives us the chance. I firmly believe that *most of the battles are battles of the mind*. Once you make up your mind, you will surely succeed...and this you realize when you meet such people.

I still recall such instances—some of them, that is—which involved my own determination. One of them is as follows...

In one of my previous organizations there was a great salesman. He had a unique ability to make a sale very quickly. No wonder, he was always highlighted in various meetings that I attended. I was in pre-sales at that time and had always admired him for his work. Since we worked for different departments, I never got the chance to meet him. And above all, *he was always on the road*. Over a period of time, I got so inspired by listening to his success stories that I started thinking of ways to meet him. For that, I first found out his domain of operation. He was in charge of one of the software products that my company had developed. Over the next 3 months, I gathered information about that product from a pre-sales standpoint—all by myself during my free time. Once I felt fully comfortable with that product, I learnt how to develop quick proof of concepts using the software. Then, I approached my manager, to give me an opportunity—somehow—to work with him in the next sales pitch. When she learnt that I had really worked hard to learn all about his 'product area,' she took pity on me and gave her approval. Within the next few weeks, *finally*, I met him. For the next 6 weeks, I utilized this huge opportunity of working with him (after which, I was back to where I belonged) and those 6 weeks were awesome 'lessons in sales' for me. They have been my guiding principles till today. Till date, I have been in close touch with him and tell him, "Whenever you need support from a die-hard fan of yours, I am just a call away!" (How I find that time, is a different story though.)

I also recall an article that I had read on one of the famous Indian movie actor who confessed, "One of the things that I focus on, is choosing the people that I need to work with. I work with only a select-set of movie directors and producers. There have been times when I had to leave huge sums on the table and say 'no' to some of the producers, simply because I cannot say 'no' to the ones I prefer to work with. I adjusted my dates to accommodate schedules for my set of preferred people. I know this has generated lot of bad press-coverage for me. But this is what I am—and I am okay with my style and individuality. I am more concerned about working with great people, and on deriving satisfaction from my work. Money has never been a criterion, even though I never say 'no' to it. ☺. And do you know, one of my preferred directors does not even pay me my market price. He tells me that I have become too expensive for him to afford! So, for him, I work with whatever he gives me. *I need him more than he needs me.* It is as simple as that. Moreover, it is always the person who is thirsty who goes to the well. The reverse never works in real life. To sum up, satisfaction and the quality of work remain my top priorities when it comes to making choices."

No wonder, he is one of the most successful actors that we have. Not from the number of hits that he has delivered, but from the perspective of giving us some classics—masterpieces—for our very own movie libraries at home.

There is another incident worth mentioning here. Many years after my graduation I got an opportunity to visit my college to hire a few fresh graduates for my company. The campus recruitments are quite tiring and time consuming. But as I evaluated kids during the day, I promised myself to take the time out to meet one of my very old professors. He taught us one of the subjects for which I used to scare myself to death. I recalled the 'n' number of scolding that usually followed his lectures—simply because I was not good at the subject, while he had set up his KRAs around making me perfect.

By the time we wrapped up the selections, it was 11 p.m. I was damn tired, and worse, had an early morning flight to catch, back home. After a careful thought, I decided to honor my commitment made during the day. I gathered courage to walk to his apartment, which was inside the college premises. I knew it was very late. So as I had already decided, I pressed the doorbell only once and waited—and would have returned had it not been opened, instead of pressing the doorbell again. But after a few minutes, I saw my teacher standing right in front of me. He was already old when he taught us. Hence, now he was 'very very' old. I too had aged, with some grey hairs showing up. I wondered if he would recognize me. But when I called him, "Sir," he instantly recognized me. He recalled my name and called me in. We spent about two hours together and when I left, he had tears in his eyes. When I was leaving, he hugged me and said, "You have given me one of the best gifts that anyone could have got on his birthday—by being with me and talking to me." It was his birthday and I felt very pleased with myself for having done the right thing—which I could, only because I had gathered the courage (remember I went at 11 p.m., and that is quite late in the night) to meet someone whom I have always admired in my life. *That day, I hugged myself* ☺.

Over the years, I have followed a lot of authors ardently and Jack Trout has been one of them. I have always admired his thoughts around branding and positioning. His writing style and the way he has bluntly written about big brand failures enamor me. And all his books (including some very rare ones)—published till date—grace my library. I keep reading them over and over again, whenever I get time. One morning, as I was going through the newspaper, I read that Jack was in Delhi for two days to conduct a workshop: on 'being a marketing warrior.' So what did I do next? You guessed it right! I attended it. It was like a dream come true to listen to someone—about whom I had been reading everything, ardently for years—face-to-face. Jack was at his charismatic best, and I was awestruck by his workshop. When the workshop ended, I went to say goodbye personally and received something that I could not have imagined even in my wildest of dreams: his latest book—which he took out from his bag, signed on the first page, and gifted to me. ☺.

Hence, if you admire someone, do yourself a favor…meet 'that' someone. Trust me. It feels good.

29 Everyone Counts

♣

When it comes to judging people, most of the times we end up making mistakes, evaluating them by their appearances, their behavior and their dressing sense. And we extend the same parameters of evaluation even to our professional lives. Thus, we judge: a company by its size and the location of its offices; a client by the amount of business that he gives; and people, by their designations, corner offices and visiting cards. Little do we realize that during such evaluations we miss one critical, yet invisible parameter, which can change the rule of the game: 'time.' In fact, I have always considered 'time' as a true game changer.

We cannot predict accurately how time will play, and thus is falsified our judgment around companies, clients and people. But, I can surely share one of the ways of surviving its heat. It involves following a simple yet powerful rule: *everyone counts*. Whether it is our personal life, or professional, the rule is applicable to each domain—and when applied, will help us deal with situations in a much better way. The underlying principle behind this rule is to see everyone with the same set of eyes; and carry the belief that no matter how small they might look, they *do* count.

> The principle asserts: do not judge them by their appearance, their size or their looks.

I have come across many people who change their behavior on

the basis of the 'designations' that they meet. They would enter into a meeting and would only talk to people who carry a 'heavier' visiting card, compared to that of others present in the room. They tend to focus only on the ones who are at the top, bypassing the juniors. In typical business meetings, I have seen their behaviors changing, the moment their visiting cards are exchanged. Either they lose interest in the meeting, simply because they don't find anyone who is as qualified in stature as they are, or they focus only on people whom they 'mentally short-listed' while exchanging introductions. However, they forget the power that 'influencers' bring on the table. The people whom you bypassed, in order to hobnob with top executives, may appear to be small, *but you never know.* They could very well end up being the ones who decide the fate of the deal that you had been pursuing for long.

It is not so hard to accept the fact that our behavior changes, the moment we come to know the designation of the person or the role that person plays in the company. If he is an SVP or a CIO, we behave differently; if he is a project manager, we behave in a different manner. Sometimes, we even let our junior folks run (and ruin) the show, simply because we don't see many senior executives on the table from the other side. However, never discount the power behind the parameter called 'time,' which can swing the game to either side.

I still recall one of the incidents, which is worth mentioning here. Years ago, one of my bosses called up a meeting that included key stakeholders like me. He had just returned from a business trip. He had met there one of his old acquaintances over a game of golf. This person was new to the world of off-shoring IT services and wanted to start a small engagement with us, to prove its benefits to his European bosses. Since he knew my boss well, he was candid enough to tell him about the size and future prospects of his proposal. It involved setting up a team of just two programmers offshore, to provide support to his systems, with no chances of expansion whatsoever. My boss was in a state of fix. He never wanted to get into such a small business; at the same time, he wanted to keep the relations amicable with this person. So, he asked each one of us if we could help him by supporting this small piece of business. Most of my folks, present in the room, did some quick calculations and came out with extremely good reasons for citing their helplessness! The reasons were: non-availability of a manager to oversee such a small project; deficient strength of management (staff); overworked managers; and lack of expertise required for delivering the project. Since it was a 'round' table meeting, I being the last, was voted as the Roman volunteer and everyone congratulated me for *taking* this project under my business unit.

When I handed over this project to one of my best managers, I told her, "I know this is going to be an overhead for both of us. But, a client is a client. Moreover, he is trying to prove how off-shoring can be beneficial to his organization. So let us ensure that we give him the same level of respect and attention that we would normally extend to a client giving us fifty times larger project than this one."

The first few months were a nightmare because the client was tough and very demanding. Some of his staff were not interested in sending work to India and hence, created all sorts of problems and challenges for us. It started consuming my bandwidth in a quantity more than what I had estimated. It was hard to believe that I was spending the amount of time that I normally would have spent on projects 50 times the size of this one. Anyways, *unlike change*, which is the only constant in life, after a few weeks of attention and hard work the project *settled* and went into a comfortable zone.

We all ensured that we stayed in touch with our client, and did not behave in a manner which would make him feel small. Months went by... And then, one day he left his organization. I set up a call to wish him the very best for the future. Life became normal again. A couple of months later, I received a message on my LinkedIn mailbox from the same person. And you know what? He wished to know if I would be interested in doing business with him. Apparently, in his new role he was much more powerful, than he was in his previous organization when we had worked together. His current portfolio was 100 times bigger than what he handled previously. Within the next few weeks we met and agreed to work together yet again.

Since we had known each other for years, we were more like friends by now. On one of the Fridays, while he was in India, I asked him, "What made you come back to me? We supported you with a *team of only two people, during those years*. What made you think that we were the best choice for supporting you, *even with such a large team now*?" He smiled, took a large sip of his beer and said, "I liked the attention you and your team extended to my project, even though you knew that it was very small and I was very demanding. That one quality gave me enough confidence, to award this large piece of work to your company. When you gave so much of attention to such a small piece of work—especially in today's world, where things get measured by nothing else but numbers—I was confident that I will get the right focus and attention from your team on this new piece of work as well." He continued with his usual smile and winked: "But don't think that my demands will go down." And we ordered another round of beer for ourselves. ☺.

That day, I realized furthermore the power that 'time' carries in 'its' palms—and how 'it' could turn out to be a real game changer for each one of us. Moreover, since we cannot predict how 'time' would behave in the future, it is always better to carry this rule in our left pocket: *"Everyone counts."*

30 Learning from the Game

♦

Cricket, in India, is almost like a religion. It is not only the most loved sport in India, at times the love converts to fanaticism!

Quite naturally, we brimmed with joy and filled pages on Facebook, congratulating 'Team India.' Yet, we could not believe that the World Cup euphoria had culminated in an equally glorious fashion: India winning the World Cup.

For me, personally, watching the classy finals led me to these learning...

1. ***Your best players can also fail.***
   More often than not, we play our most important games assuming that we will win with the help of our best players. While most of the time this turns out be true, but not always, as we cannot discount the surprise factor. We need to understand, and acknowledge, the fact that even our best players can fail. If we do not have a Plan B for such situations, then it is better to be prepared for a lost battle. Even in the corporate world, at times, we estimate our projects keeping in mind our best performers and commit to the clients based on those assumptions. I have come across such instances, when even after keeping a good contingency margin, we ran into situations where the fixed-bid projects overran their budgets far more than

the risk reserve that we had planned for. Reasons were many. But one of them definitely pertained to the core team members, who either did not live up to the expectations or left the project midway.

2. ***Do not feel pressure, when you meet unexpected failure.*** This has been explained in detail in one of the chapters later (The KYF mantra). If your key players fail to deliver, do not succumb under pressure. See this as an opportunity to do something extraordinary for your team. This is one of the most common phenomena that I have observed in my professional life. Take for example, a fixed-price project. As long as the project is 'green,' everything is green. If you look into the historical data around failures of fixed-price projects, you would notice that most of the projects met their tipping point for a 'red zone,' only a few days after they had hit the 'orange zone' for the very first time. The first week in 'orange,' and the managers start putting undue pressure on the team to deliver and bring it back to 'green'—without realizing the root cause of the issues encountered. The clients too hit the panic button, a little too early, to realize that the signals may be logically pointing to something that needs attention from the perspective of the process. Any pressure, when exerted at the wrong place and wrong time, proves fatal. As the team is forced to deliver under pressure, under such circumstances the quality gets compromised. The 'pressure' gives rise to less process-compliances, which in turn lead to more process-failures, thereby, taking the project from 'orange' to the 'red zone.' In reality, all we have to do is keep the focus intact, when the team is under pressure. The manager of the team must encourage the team, rather than putting undue pressure on it. He must *direct* the team to do what is right, in the *best possible manner*—and not make unreasonable demands, that too, in the worst possible manner.

3. ***When your best players fail, your second-in-line command must rise to the occasion.***
One of my mentors used to tell me, "We must always

hunt for situations which are complex and difficult to solve. In fact, run *towards* such situations, rather than *running away* from them. Use them to excel. Because, when you deal with such situations, you become better than the rest. Your ability to solve the problem, and propose a solution, increases multiple times. You become better with your judgments. In fact, you become a master of situations. Most of the times, you will see the team falling, as soon as the leader falls or as soon as the top two or three performers fail. It is then that a hero is required to emerge out of the rubbles, and stand up with courage to keep the flag flying high. History has proven, time and again, that heroes emerge when defeat looks imminent."

4. ***Captain takes the final call.***
   Irrespective of what the world says about collaboration, accountability and teamwork, the truth lies like the elephant in the room. It is only and only the captain, who is held responsible for the result, at the end of the game. Whether it is the captain of the team or the CEO of the company, he is the one who has to call the shots. Therefore, it is important for the team to respect and obey his decisions. During the finals, there were many moments when everybody thought that the captain took the wrong decisions. I could hear everyone shouting against him, but as the game progressed—and went in India's favor—everyone started praising the captain for the same decisions!
5. ***Taking risks is important—even when the stakes are very high.***
   It is another great learning that I acquired from the game that day. Many times, we tend to succumb under pressure, especially when the stakes are high. This happens all the time in corporate life. One good example is the prevalent conditions during the mergers and acquisitions, when I see the CEOs taking wrong decisions with respect to branding, culture and people. Rest of the times, it is either the pressure of the top line or of the bottom line, which

forces the CEOs of the companies to make the wrong choices. And sometimes, it is just the pressure exerted by the Wall Street honchos. In most of the autobiographies that I have read—of famous CEOs—one attribute common to all was their ability to make the choices which were difficult and involved doing that which was not obvious. All those great CEOs simply did what *they* thought was right, without thinking about its repercussions at the stock market or about those people who would get upset due to such decisions. History bears testimony to the fact that most of the CEOs got killed because of not taking those big risks, which were absolutely essential for their companies at one point of time or the other. They chose to be with the mindset and emotions of Wall Street, instead. Who can forget the kind of risks Steve Jobs took, while creating history—right from Pixar to iPhone. All he did was follow his passion of doing something great for his company, even if that meant upsetting his own management a number of times in the process. Believe me, it is not an easy task to accomplish at all. And that is why you have only one Steve Jobs and one Jack Welch and one Bill Gates. Now, I am not saying that we must be practitioners of the hara-kiri principle. But calculated risks, without worrying about the stakes, would always give us better results.

6. ***Take ownership of your decisions.***
   Remember always what the captain observed at the end of the game, as he mentioned the two questions that everyone would have asked if they had lost. The captain knew that he was accountable for all the decisions he took during the game. A good captain or the head of the company is ultimately the person deemed responsible for winning or losing a game—be it the playing field or the corporate battlefield. If you have read Jack Trout extensively, you will notice that one of the biggest reasons that he has attributed to corporate failures, is the inability of its CEO to concentrate on the key decisions and

adhering to them when it mattered the most. One of the managers that I worked with, in the past, was extremely good at this. He would encourage us to take risks, but always emphasized on treating those risks as our own babies. I have seen a lot of people making good use of what my boss termed as 'upward delegation.' Such people would go ahead and take a decision. However, when things went wrong, they would delegate it to their bosses to resolve. I see this as running away from the decisions they made, instead of taking ownership of the same.

7. ***Captain is still the captain of the ship, no matter how good the team is.***
I still remember my boss's words around this. He used to tell us, "No matter how good the team is, at the end of the day a team is as good as its captain." He always used to warn us against the consequences of choosing the wrong captain, whether it was a game or a project. He advised thus: "Most of the times, it is the captain who will choose you, and not the other way round. Remember, how the Sorting Hat chose Harry Potter for the 'House of Gryffindor.' This happens in our corporate life too. The Sorting Hat chooses you. But, if given a chance to choose your house, you must always choose the one which has a better 'master.' It matters not if the 'house' looks weak from outside."

8. ***Don't get impatient, no matter what!***
The lesson that we ought to learn from Gautam Gambhir's failure to complete his century: *not to be impatient*. Just when things were going fine, he became desperate and made a silly mistake and got out in the process. If we had lost that day, this particular weakness of his would have been the sole reason. We tend to forget that good things come slow in life, and only to people who know the value of patience and thus exercise perseverance. We need to respect this quality, even when we are under the greatest pressure to deliver. Do not assume this to be easy at all. Though I keep telling my

staff to be patient—whatever be the endeavor—when I face it myself, I do know how tough it is to exercise patience and calmness of mind. When the going gets tough, I remind myself of my favorite icon, Mahatma Gandhi. Just imagine, had he been impatient with the struggle for freedom, what would have happened? There were many instances when he might have felt our freedom was unattainable. But his qualities and virtues finally led the struggle to see the light of freedom. Gandhi was one leader who was not just good at it, but was actually a true master at controlling his mind and heart, no matter what!

9. ***Respect the subject matter experts.***
   Do you remember how the team members showed respect to Sachin Tendulkar, as they carried him on their shoulders while taking a victory lap? They knew it would be Sachin's last World Cup and hence, they showered their respect and honored him thus. Similarly, in each industry we have the SMEs—the 'subject matter experts.' Corporates must never forget that SMEs are the ones who are the knowledge base of the company, carrying the company on their shoulders. If your company is a product-based organization, this matter should concern you even more. Simply put, they are *the heart* of your business, no matter how good a manager you are. So shower respect and keep them happy.
10. ***Team play matters the most.***
   Remember, what was taught to us when we were in schools? "United we stand, divided we fall." Believe it or not, it still holds true—as one of the fundamental rules of, and tools for, success—in each game and in our corporate life as well. The root cause behind the success of any team is the ability of its members to work synchronously, in tandem. There may be instances where conflicts take an upper hand, but that is okay, as long as we put up a great show ultimately as a team. Differences of opinion would always remain. What is important is our ability to recognize it, deal with it and thus live with

it. My teacher used to tell me, "You cannot win battles alone—neither without an able commander nor without an equally charged army. All dots *have* to connect, to form a line. A family that eats together, stays together."

P.S. For my international readers: to learn more about the game of cricket, please visit: *http://en.wikipedia.org/wiki/Cricket.*

31 The 'HQ' Test

♥

I have always tried very hard to follow Mahatma Gandhi's principles: on being truthful, assertive, and polite, along with treating everyone and their work with respect and equality. And believe me, it is easier said than done. *I have been trying, to 'be perfect,' over these many years.* Hence, I know how tough it is to follow these principles in today's world. Yet, I know I will keep on trying till the end.

In this endeavor of mine, dignity of labor is something that I have used as a test to judge others, with respect to their HQ (humanity quotient)—and it has always worked out well for me. One of my mentors told me once: "Always remember…the true character of a man is what he is in the dark." And till date, not only I have remembered his advice, I have even followed it very seriously.

There are many situations in which we can choose to apply this simple test and judge the true character of people. And once you start doing this, you will be saddened—and hugely surprised too—to see how most of the people around us lead a superficial life, wearing multiple layers of thick make-up—of falsity. This simple test can help peel the layers of make-up and reveal his true identity. Always remember, a person will, at all times, be very close to his original colors. So, depending upon whether he passed or failed the test, you can easily understand the true nature and character of that person. Besides, his connection with his inner-self—or the lack of it—too is reflected thus.

In the following lines, I share some instances to show who passed and who failed in this test. ☺.

I used to work for a manager who was very polite in the office and was respected by everyone in the team for his softness. *I repeat, he was respected for his serene and polite nature.* I never saw him angry or shouting at anyone. So, when he failed the 'dignity of labor test,' I got the deepest shock of my life. It so happened, that one day, both of us had reached the conference hall earlier than the scheduled time for a meeting. As we were waiting, there being plenty of time still left for the meeting to start, I asked if he wanted some coffee. He affirmed. I stood up to get one for myself and expected him to do the same. But guess what? He said, "Keep sitting. Let me call this useless office boy to bring it for us. He is good for nothing and never does any work." And he dispensed with an abusive word for him, in the end. I was stunned, since the coffee vending machine was hardly 10 steps from where we sat (his HQ score started to go down). Then he dialed from the conference hall and called the boy. The moment the boy turned up, he ordered rudely, "Go, get us 2 coffees and don't delay." That day, he failed my test and his true character was unmasked. Even now, when I sometimes talk to him (just to keep in touch), I keep his HQ score at the back of my mind.

Then there is another instance, with a different outcome though. I was on a business trip to Chennai with some presentations to make. Once I had completed my office chores, I headed to one of the leading bookstores in the city (something that I always do when I have time, whether at home or while I am on business trips away from home). After spending a couple of hours and picking 3-4 good books, I headed to the billing section. There was a large queue, with an estimated lead time of maybe more than 15 minutes. Anyways, as I had nothing else to do other than heading to the airport, I was fine with the wait and started reading one of the books that I had selected, but was yet to pay for. Just then, I realized that the man standing ahead was no ordinary man. He was one of the leading movie directors, well-known for making intelligent movies. I immediately introduced myself, and appreciated his contribution towards taking Indian cinema to the international arena. Then I asked the obvious: "You could have easily gone to the top of the line, and got your billing done on priority. The store would have gladly obliged." He smiled and replied, "No. Each one, standing ahead of me, has some important work to do and their time is as important as mine. So I would prefer to wait for my turn, rather than throw tantrums and hold the store on ransom." One simple declaration and he passed the 'dignity of labor test' with high HQ scores.

Here comes another…

A few months ago, after a refreshing vacation with my family, we were waiting at the airport to take the flight back home. Since we had checked-in quite early, I was chatting with my wife when I saw someone walking towards us. And to my surprise, he was one of my super-bosses. As he greeted me, I introduced my wife and my junior. He greeted my wife and hugged my son with great love, in a manner as if he knew my family very well. Even while boarding the plane, he felt very awkward (it reflected on his face) because he was in the 'business class' and we were in 'economy' (on the other hand, I know of many people who actually boast about traveling in 'business' or 'first class,' but this guy, high on the 'HQ' score, behaved in an exactly opposite manner). Had I been alone, he would have surely done one of the two things: either upgraded me to the 'business class' or downgraded himself to 'economy.' When we reached Delhi, he was kind enough to come forward and say goodbye to us. And guess what? He even gifted my son a drawing kit (which he must have asked for, from the cabin-crew, during the course of the flight). That day, I learnt from him: how to behave when someone reaches the pinnacle of his/her career. Till date, my son remembers him. And when you can create an impression on the innocence of kids, you know you are on the right path.

All we need to do is, show some respect towards what the other person works for, no matter what that work is. Try it out. It is difficult, no doubt. But not impossible. So next time, when a telemarketer calls you to buy a loan or apply for a free credit card, don't make fun or be rude. Just politely decline his/her request and disconnect the call. I notice many people flaunting their smartness by putting the call on a speakerphone, and make fun of the person, while their friends too listen and participate. And then, after a long conversation, they disconnect the call rudely. Come on, the poor person is just doing his/her job to take care of his/her family. Moreover, no job is inferior, when done with respect.

Hence, the next time when you get into a similar situation, remember, a pair of eyes will be evaluating *your* 'HQ'...and I am sure you will want to pass your 'HQ' test with flying colors!

32 There are a Few Things that Money Can't Buy

♠

We live life on such a fast track these days that we hardly realize how weeks get converted into months and months into years, until one day, when all of a sudden we find ourselves alone...very lonely...with no one to speak to and no one to share our achievements and sentiments. It is in such a moment of revelation, that we realize, how in the blind race for success we have left a lot of things behind...which are beyond our reach now. We find ourselves at a place in time from where it is impossible to take a U-turn, and drive back to the place from where we had originally started. The bargain, that we loved at one point when we had to choose between: relations and fame; time, success and money and thus, chose: fame, success and money, starts appearing as the worst bargain that we had ever opted for.

I have come across lot of people in my life who belong to this category... People with 'fat' bank balances, yet very poor: either because they had no time to spend those hard earned dollars or they had no one on their side to share those riches with. So poor they had rendered themselves that they even forgot to bring flowers during those special days of their life...*and so poor, that they could not afford to fly down, when their parents needed them the most—during their last few days on earth.*

I have come across globetrotters, who boasted about having seen half of the world and pocketed millions of air miles to their credit, yet were so myopic that they failed to watch their kids' very first steps; failed to count the countless hours, their spouse and kids spent at the dinner table, waiting for them to join (while they were busy attending those deal-clinching boardroom meetings); failed to shower those flying kisses, on seeing their kids dressed up like fairies and pirates, while participating in those annual day functions; and failed to jump with joy on seeing those trophies their kids brought back home. *In fact, effectively they failed to be a part of all that matter the most in life.*

Achievers, who were epitomes of success—and were once famous for never missing their targets—missed miserably on all that matters. Though physically present, yet virtually absent (busy typing messages on their smartphones), while watching those weekend movie shows, they missed out on all the enjoyment. They were so deft, yet missed out on encouraging their kids and sending those "Best of luck" cards, when they fought the battles of their life. So attentive to detail in professional matters they were, yet missed watching the details around how their kids grew up all those years...and thus missed out on all priceless sights, and associated memories that they had left far too behind.

They are such winners, who won a lot of those 'stocks,' fame and success for themselves, yet lost heavily on their health. So strong on asset management they turned out to be, yet so weak in managing their very own asset—their 'body'—they proved to be.

This truth is so evident...only if we realize it in time before our time runs out, leaving us with a big silo for the rest of our lives.

Well, these observations are *not at all only spiritual*. It is a fact that the material world too corroborates: *there are indeed certain things that money cannot buy*. It is actually the *ultimate truth* of life in this physical plane. One has to acknowledge this fact; it is only a matter of time, as the fact cannot be ignored for long. But till such time, people keep running after the superficial. Hence, most of the times, you would see people happily missing their 'life's bus' and opting for 'luxury car'—only to live with a guilt later, consumed by a 'half life syndrome.' It is a guilt that no time machine can ever reverse!

Try out these time-tested observations someday. Go ahead

and ask a very successful person about what he missed in his/her life. The response would never be: luxury cars, exotic properties or designer clothes. It would always be related to their life: life, which they could have lived and cherished well; life, which they found to be a void when they sat thinking about it years later. Yet, it was they, themselves, who had created the void, not life. Life gave them those rare opportunities when they could hear the heartbeats of their parents, soul mate and their kids. Life gave them ample scope to enjoy the fun-filled moments...and life gave them much more... And all these they wistfully acknowledge to have missed, with wrenching feelings of remorse.

Here is what one of my friends says about life and its associated price tag...

> "One of the things that I want to do in my life is to live it fully. I may not be rich as per the conventional parameters; but I can confidently boast of friends and my family who make each day of my life a very special one. My best friend is now my wife. We share our happiness, and we grieve together. I know I have a shoulder to cry on, and I also know that I have strong shoulders to allow my friends and family to lean on. I see most of the people preparing a wish-list of activities that they plan to do, once they retire. But the truth is: there is nothing called retirement, and therefore, the time after the retirement will never come. All you need to do is reinvent yourself, and start re-living your life the way *you* love to—and not the way the world would want you to. The real retirement is when you finally leave this world. I am happy that when I lie on my deathbed, just about to retire, I will be surrounded by all the relations that I invested in for so many years. Such a view would allow me to leave this world peacefully and willfully."

On this note, I end the chapter with an apt quote—**Steve Jobs'** definition of life and the things that mattered the most to him:

"Remembering that I'll be dead soon is the most important tool I've ever encountered, to help me make the big choices in life. Because almost everything—all external expectations, all pride, all fear of embarrassment or failure—these things just fall away in the face of death, leaving only what is truly important."

33 Mentoring Matters

♣

It was a sad day at the office for me, and that happens rarely. Failures have never affected me and there is nothing called 'bad news' in my dictionary. Hence, such things could never be the cause of my sadness. The last time that I was sad was when I had lost my father.

The reason behind the sadness on this particular day was related to my mentor—my greatest mentor—whom I was about to lose. He was leaving the company and it was his last working day at the office.

Before I share my feelings related to this incident, let me confess that I see the word 'mentoring' or 'mentor' being overused in the corporate sector these days, without really understanding its true essence. As with leadership, most of the people feel as if mentoring flows in their blood. If that had been the case, by now we would have had many Gandhis and many more Bill Gates'. If I close my eyes and count the number of people whom I could place in the category of good mentors, I know I would need only one hand to complete the count.

During all these years we had shared a great teacher-student-friend kind of relationship. I still remember the day when he decided to shift to another company. That day, he had called me up and discussed the new opportunity that had come his way. After he explained it in detail, he expected an honest opinion. I must admit, it was a difficult one. My 'right brain' wanted to behave selfishly, and dissuade him from embracing the opportunity. But as always, my 'left brain' took charge: I declared that it would be better for him to take up the new assignment. After submitting his resignation, he immediately called me to inform that the countdown had begun. And soon I realized that the notice period he had served had flown by—just like daughters, who grow up so fast that even before you realize they are married and settled.

Working with him had been fun—besides being a huge learning experience—over all these years. He would make me laugh; he would coach me on how to do things in the right manner; and he would subtly tell me in private where I had erred, without hurting my feelings. Under his guidance and leadership, I grew as a good human being, above everything else. He taught me: how to enjoy complex situations, how to take the right decisions and live by them, how to handle and kiss failures…and much more…

He used to always tell me, "Making the right kind of associations and working with good mentors must be the only concerns in your career. If you are in the company of good mentors, you will always be at your efficient best, attaining the highest productivity levels. And to top it all, you will enjoy doing what you do. They will fill your life with energy levels that only winners experience."

Heart controls the mind at times, and when that happens, emotions take control of your body. On his last working day, I experienced the same. I fumed with frustration that he was leaving me in the lurch and moving. I also experienced loneliness, with thoughts raging within: *"With whom I would share my pains? Who will guide me now? What will happen if I make mistakes?"* I experienced anxiety and pain...and I felt tears rolling down my cheeks. I decided not to meet him and hence, chose to maintain a distance. I thought it would make life easier for me, at least for that day. And it did. He left. I knew I could never face him, to bid him goodbye—*because by then, he was a mentor for me...for life.*

It reminded me of a beautiful quote by **Albert Schweitzer**:

> "In everyone's life, at some time, our inner fire goes out. It is then burst into a flame by an encounter with another human being. We should all be thankful to all those who rekindle the inner spirit."

And truly, mentors are the ones who ignite that inner spirit, which is much needed to re-invent us in the corporate world continuously, and thus sustain ourselves vibrantly.

Years have passed by and I have found many new mentors in life's beautiful journey. But 'this' mentor will always have a special place in my heart. You know what? Since we *connect* almost once a month, so, though he is out of sight, but in reality, is never out of my mind. ☺.

34 Have you Tasted a Blowfish Yet?

♦

'Blowfish sushi' is something to die for! I mean it literally. But you won't want to be savoring a piece of this delicacy before you have all relevant facts. Just remember, if your sushi chef slips in its preparation, the game will be over even before it begins!

Before I divulge further, let me tell you that this incident is going to be an interesting read for everyone. And for me, it contains some special memories—and one of the greatest lessons of my life.

Years ago, I managed a client in Japan, in the capacity of an 'engagement relationship manager' stationed in India. However, I used to travel once in a while, to ensure that there were no showstoppers, owing to differences in culture and language. Hence, they were happy with our services.

During one of those business trips, I happened to meet their CEO. (In fact, he extended the invitation since we had done some great work for them, pulling their project out of the 'red zone.') He appreciated the hard work of my team in reaching the difficult milestones. Furthermore, he commended us on our work ethics and quality of deliveries, even while working under extreme pressure. Getting a pat on the back for ethics and quality, from a Japanese client, is like a dream come true for any working executive.

A day before heading back home, I received a call from the CEO's assistant. She told me that the CEO wanted to take me out for dinner and asked if I had any preferences. Honestly, I wasn't expecting something of this nature just a day before my tenure ended there. Excited at this opportunity to share some quality time with the CEO, I rushed with my answer without giving it a proper thought (that I was in Japan and not a great fish-eater), and said, "No preferences." Prompt came the reply from the other side, "There is a new sushi bar in town and it is known for its blowfish delicacies. I am booking a place for two." (It was only later that I found the CEO had a special liking for blowfish.)

I had never visited a sushi bar before. Hence, blowfish was something that I heard for the first time. Subsequently, I opened my laptop and 'Yahooed' to search what a sushi bar would look like, and what a blowfish was (Google hadn't arrived into the cyber world then). Out of all that was written on the web, pertaining to the subject, lines that caught my attention were:

> The blowfish, or 'Fugu' as it is known in Japanese, contains a nasty poison called Tetrodotoxin. An amount, just the size of a pin-head, is enough to kill one person. The fish in itself contains enough poison to kill as many as 30 people! So what happens if you eat an ill-prepared blowfish sushi? Well, the poison will paralyze your muscles, while you remain fully conscious. Death, by suffocation, occurs within a few hours. Some of the symptoms of eating poisonous blowfish sushi include: a numb tongue, lips and face—as also, dizziness and vomiting.

The excitement of having dinner with the CEO, which had peaked only moments ago, evaporated on reading these words. While the web mentioned numbness of the tongue as one of the symptoms of eating a bad blowfish, I felt the same numbness within; as if words had left my mouth, before they could even touch my tongue. The next thought that came to my mind was to ring up my wife and speak to her (one last time,☺). After reading all that I had, I thought I was just a couple of hours away from kissing my death. Death seemed imminent! So, I did call my wife and spoke for a few minutes, not knowing what to speak. Then I took a shower, and dressed to look good. God! I was so stupid. (I laugh much, every time I recall this now, especially at my immaturity and thus, stupidity around this episode.)

On arriving at the sushi bar, I found the CEO already waiting for me, even though I was a few minutes earlier than the designated hour. (That is Japanese work ethics for you, my friends!) Our conversation began, encompassing the current project and some other potential opportunities. And then, finally, came this guy with a menu card and an order book. Without even looking at the menu card, the CEO ordered Sashimi. (I remember the dish was very costly during those days: around 100$.) I mumbled, "What a way to die... You pay so much, only to eat something that has the potential to kill you even." I was clueless as I sat at the bar, and it was very much apparent on my face; at least that is what he guessed, as he looked at me. Before he could speak, I said with full ignorance, "I am okay with sushi as well." (I thought Sashimi was some kind of sushi.) He smiled and said, "No, no. I ordered a blowfish dish for both of us. This place is pretty famous for it."

Just like the countdown that begins before the launch of a shuttle, my own countdown—to death—had begun. I was nervous and it was obvious from the pallor of my face. Finally, the dish arrived. But before we could start, the CEO said, "Do you know why I brought you to this place? It is 'trust' that brings us to this place. In our lives, we only need 'trust' to do the work for us. Human beings tend to think far more than what is required. Most of the times, we 'over think' and make life complicated—for ourselves as well as for others."

He looked into my eyes, pointed to the dish and continued...

"We all know that this fish can kill us if it is not prepared correctly. Yet, you will see in a short while from now, that you will survive. Why? Because you trusted and believed in the highly seasoned chef who has been issued a license only after a 3-year long apprenticeship. The licensing exam consists of: a written test, a fish-identification test, and a practical test that involves preparing and eating the fish. And you know what? Only 35% of them are issued this license. We all know that this fish could kill us. Still we eat and enjoy eating this, because we put trust before anything else. Similarly, in the corporate world, we entrust you with projects which are worth millions of dollars. We all know that one mistake in the execution of the projects, and we lose the money. Yet, we give you those projects. Why? Because, we trust you. We believe in what you do, and we know that we will survive and relish those projects, just like the way we survive and relish our 'Fugu.' So go ahead and relish your meal."

Little did he realize that in the process, he had taught me one of priceless lessons of life.

Since then, whenever I have to entrust someone with assignments that involve high risks and stakes, I remember this incident and see if the person has a 'trust factor' of '10 out of 10.' Because I know deep within, if that is the case, we all will survive—and relish them too. ☺.

Note: Few more words on Sashimi...

A very popular dish, it has so thin slices that the pattern of the plate can be seen through the fish. Knives, with exceptionally thin and sharp blades, are used for cutting blowfish into these translucent slices; and the technique is known as Usuzukuri. These plates are often decorated in the form of a Chrysanthemum: a flower, which has a huge significance in Japanese culture.

35 Royal Empires

♥

I always acknowledge that my 11-year old son has been one of my best teachers on the subject of "Life." The reasons behind my love for attending his classes: there are no scheduled classes; no boring lectures I am subjected to; there no theories, only practical, which you can learn on the run; and they are for free, since he does not charge anything for his classes. ☺. And more than anything else, the manner in which he delivers the lessons is simply enamoring.

Of late, he has picked up a game, *Royal Empires*, on the internet, for which his friends join him remotely.

One day, he came to me and said, "Daddy, I need to buy some 'special soldiers pack' for building my army, in order to defend my empire. It will cost us 4.99$." I looked at him, went to his computer to enter my credit card information, and bought his desired 'pack.'

After a week, he came back again and iterated, "Daddy, I need another one, because those special soldiers died." I looked at him again, and saw his face beaming with enthusiasm, clearly reflecting his level of interest in the game. Hence, another pack was bought.

A week later, he dropped in with the same request, but this time with a twist in the plot: "Daddy, my friends have told me that they run 'crazy Fridays' promotions, to give *more* for the same amount of money. So let us buy on a Friday this time." I wore a serious look and asserted: "Okay. But you seem to be investing

5 dollars to this crazy game every week, and that is too much of money for me."

Instant was his innocent reply, "No daddy, it is just 4.99$ (as if the exchange rate between Indian Rupees and US Dollars was 1:1)."

I smiled, but while buying, told him grimly this time, "Listen, no more spending on this game. Find a new game, which does not ask for so much money every week. I am filling your army for the last time now."

He nodded in agreement, and just like kids carry their cute innocence, ran away to play again.

A week passed and I waited for him to come back. But he did not. Then another week passed. I waited, thinking: maybe, he would come with the 'crazy Friday' kind of a deal. Still he did not come. By the time the third week had passed, it was too much of a suspense for me. So I went ahead and asked him, "How is your game going on these days? Have you got a new game to play on the internet?"

He looked at me curiously and replied, "No. I am playing the same game."

On learning this, I asked, "Is it? But then, how are you managing your armies without that extra money, which you were spending earlier every week?"

He stood up, as if he was about to explain to me the logic behind a complex algorithm, and replied, "Daddy, I stopped buying those special soldiers. You were right. They were taking too much of my money every week. So, I invested in training my soldiers using the gold that I earned, rather than spending it on building an army of special soldiers. It is working well, for now."

Little did he realize that he had *taught me* a great lesson in the process.

I remembered, how at times we spend a lot of money in hiring those costly expensive resources for their special skills, and forget about building them in a cost-effective manner which can be accomplished by cross-training and certifications. If this is restricted only to consulting, I can understand the reason behind it. But in a typical setup, we should never undermine the power of training and developing people upwards.

I accept that choosing between experience and training is

always a tough call, simply because experience will help you almost instantaneously in getting the work done—while training people, for the same job, takes time. However, the art lies in taking a long-term view of the game and then play. The one aspect that I have always noticed, with regards to preferring experience over training, is the inability of the former to move up the value-chain. They are rather content with their current skills. Such people hardly show the zeal to learn something new and grow. They are least inclined to do more than they are capable of. And their reluctance proves that they are least bothered about enhancing their capabilities. I have also found it tough to keep such people motivated over a longer period of time. On the other hand, when you develop talent, you might be short on experience, but definitely high on moving them up the value-chain—at the same time, in keeping them motivated.

I recall an incident when one of my managers had goofed up on my finances by hiring costly staff, in order to start new projects quickly. Only after a year had passed did he realize that while he was successful in running the project, he made very little margins due to higher operating costs.

During a meeting with one of my premier business partners once, both of us felt the need to increase our footprints in one of the niche set of skills that we operated in. The 'country manager' of that company shared a brilliant observation that day. He said, "There are only three players who operate in this niche market, and that includes you. Every time I go to any one of you and ask for additional staff, all you people do is hire from the market. Since the market has only three players, you end up eating each other's flesh, which does not help me at all. Because, while one of you gives me the human reinforcements, the other one shares the bad news of having lost the same. I have so much business on the table that I want all of you to *eat that meat, rather than each other's flesh*. The only way to accomplish this is to create a pool of talented people, and invest in training them to pick these niche skills."

P.S. Gauging *my interest* level in *his game*, my son thought of raking a mullah and declared, "Daddy, I just came to know that their would be a mega sale on Thanksgiving, and another one on Christmas. So, I will remind you to buy a few of those 'special soldiers pack' during that time." ☺.

36 Live for Greatness

♠

As has been mentioned earlier, the famous series: *The Karate Kid*, is another movie that tops my list of inspirational movies. The movie moves through many such sequences which forward significant "Life lessons." For me, the movie takes the student-teacher relationship to a completely different level, as Mr. Han (Jackie Chan) teaches his 12-year old student, Dre Parker (Jaden Smith), that kung fu is not about punches and parries but an art of maturity and calmness.

For those who have not seen this movie, let me give a quick review. It is the story of Dre and his master, Han, and the challenge they take-up: to fight in the kung fu tournament, against the very talented but ruthless kid, Cheng, and his equally brutal master, Li.

During the course of the tournament, the less on confidence Dre, was slow to achieve parity with his opponents. But soon, he began defeating them, and advanced to the semifinals—as did Cheng too, crushing his opponents brutally. Dre is eventually pitted against Liang: another of master Li's students, who is instructed by master Li to break Dre's leg. Though Liang insists that he can beat Dre, master Li sternly tells him that he doesn't want Dre to be beaten, but broken.

As the match progresses, Liang delivers a devastating kick on Dre's leg, following it up with a series of brutal punches. Although Liang is disqualified for his illegal strikes, Dre is incapacitated. This was exactly what master Li had planned as he thought it would allow Cheng to win—by default.

However, the movie takes a dramatic turn, when Dre refuses to retire. Instead, he fights back—despite all odds—and wins, defeating Cheng. And this victory over Cheng is not just a physical victory, but mental too. In the process, he earns the respect of Cheng, who finally comes forward and hands over the trophy to Dre himself.

And then comes the climax: a 'scene stealer moment.' After the awards ceremony, the Dragons Team—the losers—headed by Cheng, abandons their coach, master Li, and bows to master Han.

Do you know why these kids opted for Han? Because they realized that master Han was ethical and believed in fair practices. They also understood that a team is as good as its leader, coach, mentor, master, teacher. The Dragons realized that Dre had won because he had the 'right' master on his side: a master who possessed the right kind of qualities required in a coach, for his students to excel. He was a teacher who knew exactly what to instill in the young brains of his students. A true master is the one, to whom, losing and winning does not matter. This was what Han was. What mattered the most to him was: *to be focused on the goal and to be ethical*. He taught his students to put the best foot forward, without worrying about the results. And above all, he instilled respect for the game, guiding his student(s) to participate in tournament(s) in its true spirit. *Master Han lived for greatness and not for fame.*

As Robin Sharma defines this moment: "Greatness comes from beginning something that does not end with you." Leadership is not about being famous but about being great. You need to be ethical, fair in your judgment and treat everyone with respect—even if it is your competitor in the corporate battlefield.

Jack Welch, yet another favorite of mine, takes us a step further with his observation: "Before you are a leader, success is all about growing yourself. But when you become a leader, success is all about growing others." No wonder, Jack is widely respected for his greatness, cutting across industries and continents.

Many a times, I have noticed that people approach the right

leaders within the organization, to get an opportunity to work with them. They flock to the right leaders in the herd. Because, deep within, they know it is the right path to walk, as it would make them better individuals at the workplace. They know that only the great leaders will give them the honest feedback about their weaknesses. Realizing the weaknesses and acting upon the same, is what Darwinian theory recommends for corporate survival. No wonder, we notice mass 'movements' when a respected leader of an organization leaves!

It reminds me of one of my uncles, who retired gracefully and with much élan. He retired as the chairman of the company he worked for. That day, after the farewell party held in his honor, he spoke to me at length about his experiences in life.

One of the things that he stated was, "See, the mere thought of retiring from your work sends a shiver down your spine. You start thinking: what you will do after you retire; how will you spend time, rather, how would you kill time; how will the society react; will the young see any value in spending their time with you...and the like.

The key, however, is to accept such truths of life very gracefully and adapt thus. The board of directors wanted me to stay for at least few more years. They wanted to benefit from my rich experience. But I told them that while my experiences could be rich, my brain is not. The market needs a fresh perspective for doing business today. With the technology changing—almost on a daily basis—the experience factor has taken a back seat, while freshness of ideas has occupied all the front seats. Come on... You don't expect those fresh ideas to come from an elderly person like me. So coming back to the discussion on retirement, when you retire from the company that you served for so long, you must retire with respect. You must enthrone the right heir before you exit. You must spend considerable time in mentoring that person, so that when you are no longer with the company, the company still misses you and remembers you for your greatness—and at the same time, functioning of the company is not hampered. People must remember you for all the right reasons and for leaving a rich legacy behind, while you lay asleep in your grave."

These are indeed great thoughts of a great person.

I must refer here to another incident: the decision of the chief mentor of Infosys to retire. To me, it was one of the most graceful exits that I would ever see. It could come only from a leader of his stature. The great leader that he is, he chose his own 'exit date.'

On being asked as to what he will do after stepping down from the helm, he said: "My son too asked the same question. And I answered that *I deserve to take it easy. If I want to go to my home-office I will go. When I want to read I will read. I don't believe in the concept of second innings.*"

And that is what I call: 'living for greatness.'

P.S. "Live For Greatness" is a famous advertisement campaign of the Rolex brand, involving Roger Federer; and it is a registered trademark for Rolex Watch USA Inc.

37 | Die for Greatness

♣

When I finished writing the chapter, "Live for greatness," little did I know that I would write another chapter on greatness, but with an altogether different perspective...and all because of a recent experience.

During all these years of my marital bliss, I have picked up many good habits—and thoughts—from my wife.

Let *me* share one of her thoughts that *she* often shares with me... "We must ensure that we *are always* there for our society, our relationships and the people for whom we care, when they need us the most. There are times when we are called upon to be a part of someone's celebrations. We should try to attend them. But if we can't, it is alright. However, if our friends and acquaintances are going through a bad phase, have had a death in their family, or someone is terminally ill or hospitalized, then we must take the time and be with them. You know why? Because they need us more during such days, compared to the celebration parties during the good times."

To be very honest, there have been such occasions, when due to my work load I tried my level best to run away from my wife's principles and hence, came up with lot of creative excuses. But guess what? When you have married a girl of your choice, that too after a long courtship, you hardly get a chance to put on that 'chameleon skin' and survive with your lame excuses!

So I had to attend a funeral, of someone whom my wife knew

very well from her office days. He had recently retired from his services, and chosen to spend the rest of his time serving the underprivileged. I had met him on few occasions, during the good old days at her office get-togethers and at other celebrations. My remembrance of him was vague, though. At the funeral procession and the subsequent prayer meeting, I heard many people stand up and speak great things about this person. Someone mentioned how he had helped others during their bad days; while there were others who confessed how earnestly they wanted to thank him for his good deeds, and had missed out on the same, since he was no more. And then, there were some, who shared instances when he had come forward at the time they needed it the most. The rest, simply regretted his absence from their lives.

This whole episode made me ponder and ask myself...

"Why do we have to wait for someone to die, to share how we felt about the person? Why do we have to wait for their death to declare them great? Do we really need to die *for* greatness? Why does an autobiography top the charts, when it is released after the person is no more?"

These questions had every reason to knock at the door of my consciousness. Because, if that person had made such great impact on their lives, why didn't they thank him when he was alive? Did they ever tell him, how greatly they had been benefited by him, and how much meaning he brought to their lives? Did they show how thankful they were for his mere existence on this planet? Did they ever give him a bear hug for being there for them when they needed it the most? Did they ever stop by the florist's, and gift him a bouquet for spreading his fragrance in their lives?

You might have noticed that *we, as humans, are more accepting of someone's greatness or good deeds, only when the person is no more.* When they exist, we hardly notice people talking about them, leave aside acknowledging their good deeds. But the moment they are no more, you would see the same set of people describing their greatness in public forums, at meetings...and in general. These people would stand during their funeral, as a mark of respect, and speak highly about them.

Why?

Can't we just do the same, when the person is still alive and waiting to hear all those good words from us? After all, it wouldn't cost us more than a few hours of our lives. How about trying our best to make them feel great while they are alive, no matter which age group they belong to? Because, greatness can be achieved at any age, place or work. *Greatness knows no barriers. The barriers lie within us, as the barriers of the mind*. Thus, barriers are created and experienced by not baring our hearts—by not pouring out our emotions—for the person we love, respect and care.

Another recent example that comes to my mind is Steve Jobs' demise. While I have always been his huge fan, I know of people who declared him an eccentric, a jerk or a nut. But when he left, I noticed the same set of people talking highly about his inventions and his greatness at Apple.

So next time, if you feel great about people who (have) touched your life in some way, do not wait till their deathbed—or till they are dead—to declare them great. Express your feelings while they are alive and let them live for greatness.

38 The Gift from God!

On a chilly winter evening, we drove to a venue that had been booked for a small get-together—for and by—some of my wife's colleagues. Her office had undergone restructuring on a large scale recently. As a result, most of her office staff had changed. So, all of them had collectively decided to host a small after-office dinner, which would give them an opportunity to know each other better. Spouses were invited as well; so I tagged along!

After a few rounds of snacks, the discussion turned towards how each one's kid was doing in life. Some were happy to declare that their kids were progressing very well and were graduating from some of the finest colleges in India. Others complained about the tough road that lay ahead for their kids, before they could settle down in life. Some showed concern at their kids not being serious at all—about choosing a career for themselves; while some spoke about their changing habits, and the resultant generation gap.

While most of us expressed our thoughts openly, there was one gentleman, in his late-forties, who sat very quiet in one corner. I noticed him, engrossed in some deep thought. He was listening to all observations intently. In order to give him a chance to speak, I stepped forward and interjected, "Hang on folks. Can we give a chance to the gentleman sitting at the corner? It seems, we have been ignoring him for quite some time now. This discussion has to cover everyone. Sir, what are your thoughts around your kids?"

On being called upon, he was stunned. More so, as he would have never expected a person like me—a stranger—to stand up and speak on his behalf. My intentions were genuine, as I never want anyone to feel as if they are being ignored.

He paused for a while, gathered his thoughts, and started, "For me, this very thought—of how my kids were doing—never came to my mind. The last 17 years of my life have taught me to take things as they come. If you expect more from life, you always end up getting less! All I want to say is that I have a wonderful family to look up to, and I am happy the way I am living my life now."

All of us became quiet for a while, yet his response was quite disquieting. To me, his response did not make any sense (in the context of the discussions that we were having); and it seemed everyone else too felt the same. One of the colleagues of my wife broke the silence, as he asked, "How come you came alone today? We wanted to meet your spouse as well."

He smiled at us and replied, "The last 17 years have taught us how to lead a life, living in a family, yet being alone. So when we go to the functions, it is either my spouse or me; but we hardly attend them together." He stopped again, and with that rose our curiosity even more. And this time he sensed it, looking at our faces. From what I could understand, he was a very quiet guy who spoke little, and 'to the point.' It looked like he did not want us to go deeper into his personal life. Upon sensing the same, I tried to change the topic in a bid to respect his privacy, saying, "My son is crazy about video games, and he makes me poorer every week by buying them in tons!"

But my attempt to lighten the environment failed... I was late. I realized that the arrow had already left the quiver. The gentleman gathered courage and continued, bypassing my light comment about my son, "I have a daughter who is 17 years old, and a son who is 23 now. My wife works for a private firm as an executive assistant. Years ago, when my wife delivered a baby girl, we thanked God for being so kind to us. We were a perfect family and enjoyed being parents to a boy and a baby girl. But after her second birthday, my daughter started having bouts of fever on a continual basis. We got her examined by many doctors, and finally went in for a detailed check-up. Little did we know that the biggest shock of our lives was waiting in the backyard for us. The doctors declared that she had a rare type of blood cancer. On hearing this news, my wife fainted and I was speechless for hours. It was something which we had never expected to afflict a 2-year old child. Digesting this truth, which took more than a week, I gathered my senses and went back to the doctors to find out about her chances of survival. Even after darkest of nights, we do wake up to be greeted by bright mornings. The same was experienced: the doctors declared that her chances of survival were bright, even though it may take years and would cost a lot of money. I was so happy to hear this news that I literally went ahead and hugged him. The week—prior to this life-affirming response from the doctor—both me and my wife had lost all hopes. So this news appeared as God's direct intervention. It seemed as if God, Himself, had gone ahead and re-injected life in all of us."

By now, it was pin-drop silence in the room. The atmosphere had suddenly changed and everyone was anxious to hear more. He continued... "The happiness was short-lived as we met reality soon after. On one hand, we were financially not well-off and on the other, the whole treatment was going to take a lot of our time, since she was just a 2-year old baby. Taking into consideration all the challenges, my wife decided to take up a job, irrespective of the salary she was offered. We shifted our son from a private school to a government-run unit, cut down all expenses that we could. It included selling my car and buying a used two-wheeler, instead. Then came the huge factor of time that had to be devoted for her treatment. And in the midst of all this, it was essential that we attended to our son as well. All of a sudden, he grew up by years in maturity, belying his physical age. He understood our issues and stood by us.

Further to this, I *have* to acknowledge a fact: at times when the going gets tough, God does send angels to help you deal with such situations. The first angel came in the form of my boss. He allowed me flexible hours, without compromising on my salary.

This made life a lot easier for me. My wife had a tough job, but we had no choice. It was paying us well and we badly needed the money. So I told her to concentrate on her job, while I took care of rest of the stuff."

I could see his eyes were already wet, but he carried on... "Over the next few years, we sold our house and took many loans. Some of my friends also supported us through the thick and thin. They helped me with as much money as they could, and I never said no. I was not in a position to say no, since I badly needed money—and lots of it. By now, our daughter was going to school, which was another great responsibility at hand. Due to repeated chemotherapy sessions, she had lost all her strength and thus, had become very weak. But like all of us, she was a fighter. She always smiled back when I used to see her off at the school, leaving her under the guidance of her brother. A brother, who never went out to play; looked after his little weak sister when we worked late at the office; and a brother who never demanded any toys from us, ever. I still remember two very difficult situations that added to our woes, while we were fighting this long battle. At one point, her bone marrow dipped to such a level that she could not even walk by herself. I had to literally carry her everywhere in my arms, while she used to worry about her exams all the time. And then there was the other one: in a bid to help his mother, my son went out alone to the market to buy some readymade snacks and met with an accident. He fractured his leg, and that added to the complexities of our life. The small boy had grown immensely over the years. But we hardly realized it, till he was bedridden. His love for his family was unconditional, and he never troubled us even once during those days. All he wanted was to get his sister back to the good old days. For years, I could not cry—because I knew that if I cried, the whole family would fall like a house of cards."

By now, tears had started rolling down his cheeks, which he gently wiped, put up a brave smile and affirmed, "After so many years, it is *now* that we have settled down. My daughter is 17 and is doing well. She has had to skip many of her classes at school due to her treatment. But to me, she is a fighter. One of us is still required to be with her all the time. So now you all know, where my wife is *right now*. My son has got into a multinational firm and is earning well. Both of us are still paying off the loans that we took years back. But with my son on my side—now supporting financially as well—it looks easier than before. When you all were discussing your families, I did not know what to state. My life has gone through so many twists and turns that I no longer expect anything from it. For me, having my family with me is a gift in itself... For me it is truly **'the gift' from God**...and I am grateful for this wonderful gift called **'family.'**"

39 | Have Guts...Bell the Cat!

♥

I grew up reading Aesop's fables and one of the stories that I liked much was "Bell the cat." Like all of his fables, this one too inspires one to attempt a seemingly difficult task.

And if you apply this story to the corporate world, you will realize that not many people fit the bill. Usually we find comfort in 'being politically correct,' rather than trying to do things which are difficult and require lot of guts. Of all the people that I have met or worked with, I remember only a handful of them who had the guts to bell the cat. Rest of them belonged to the 'applaud' category. They would be very happy to hear an idea, but extremely apologetic when it came to implementing the same.

To me, belling the cat is a phenomenon pertaining to your ability to absorb and speak the truth—no matter how bitter it is. It works both ways. People who have been able to absorb hard truths, are the ones who would never hesitate in spitting it out without any fear.

One of the attributes that I have picked up, after reading Gandhi extensively, is to have the guts and share the truth. It doesn't matter how hard the truth is. The category to which the truth belongs—personal or professional—too doesn't matter. A truth is a truth and the faster you realize it, the better for you—and for all those who are somehow related to it. By shifting the dots you can increase or decrease the intensity of the truth; but the truth in itself cannot be shifted at all.

I remember an incident worth mentioning here. There came a time when one of the companies that I used to work for, went into deep financial trouble. They were not selling (due to some wrong strategies at the topmost level) and some of their existing business also went away, leaving everyone in a very tight budget situation. Such occurrences—when some quarters are good and some are bad—are perceived as very normal these days, *but in those days* it was something totally unheard of. And then the management decided not to do annual appraisals. They had no money and they were not doing good; so it made sense.

When I shared this news with my direct reports they were perturbed, but understood. We were left with two choices: accept the decision or shift base. My team though realized that they had a larger issue at hand. But at the same time, when I told them to pass it onto *their* teams, they were hesitant. Some of them came back with an idea to keep it a low-key affair and let people know by themselves; others just raised concerns that some key people might leave on hearing this. They were not completely wrong. I knew this was a critical issue, and could have a damaging impact on some huge projects that we were running. While I understood their concerns, I could not accept their idea to keep it a low-key affair. Upon seeing a lot of hesitation from my team, I told them, "I will bell the cat. Prepare a list of folks who are critical of the decision and who would be badly impacted with this decision, and then send it to me." When I got the list, I invited all of them to a dinner at an especially reserved, private dining place with a lot of space—and with lot of time at our disposal to have some heart-to-heart talk, in an informal environment.

Soon I was with all of them, having a drink, in an 'unofficial' environment. I did not invite any of my direct reports to that dinner deliberately. After a while, I took them through our company's performance, and told them how we were badly impacted in the market due to it. Some were surprised to hear of it, as I too was surprised—to know that they were living so far from the reality. Later I realized that like most of the companies, my company also had made the same mistake: of being the first to share the good news and the last to share the bad ones. The dinner went on. I knew this was not going to be an easy one. I also knew that no preparations were needed from my side, since all I was doing was showing them the truth—albeit in an attractive package. I was also aware that 'this' dinner would be discussed the next day, with larger teams: at recreation spots, over smoking sessions, over tea, at lunch and during team meetings. Some of them listened patiently. Others spitted back. Calm and patient, I listened to all of them. There were some issues raised by them with which I agreed. And then there were views with which I did not agree: those were politely turned down.

As I shared this truth, I passed the key messages: how important they were to me; how their patience and support shown to the management, now, could go a long way in taking their relationship with the company to a new level; how we can—together—convert these bad days into the good ones for the future; how we must come closer like a family and deal with it, by staying together; how their reaction could make or break things...and more, on these very lines.

Even before I began, I did let them know that there would be a few of them who would not relate or agree to what I was about to tell them. I assured them that if they felt that way, it was perfectly alright. Furthermore, I made it absolutely clear that I didn't intend to impose my views on anyone. They were requested to just respect each other's viewpoints and sentiments.

The dinner ended at midnight. I felt light and was much relieved—as if I had just completed a confession at a church. It was little premature to gauge how my extended team felt about the whole thing. Since I wanted them to chew upon this, for a little longer, I had kept this dinner on a Friday—allowing them the much needed time, over the next two days, to think about it. By the time the dinner ended, I could see a few clearly dissatisfied folks (I took a note of them, because I knew they were disconnected and would leave soon), a few neutral ones (I noted them down too, as I decided to meet them once more, the following week—separately—to convert them into positive cases), and the rest were found to be fully positive. I could *smell* their satisfaction in the fact that they had learnt about something bad, right from the horse's mouth, rather than hearing it in the corridors.

They felt important enough as they were confided in, with the *bad news—which* they had always thought, and assumed, *was to be discussed* in the boardrooms, and not in the open—with them. Some of them felt closer to the company. It seemed to them that the company had put some additional responsibility on their shoulders, by passing on this news to them in the best possible manner.

As days passed by, some of the folks that I had made note of, actually left; while there were some who made my life even easier than I could have ever imagined. They managed to make their teams understand why the company took the decision that it took. As far as I was concerned, I just followed the moral in the age-old Aesop's fable: *"Someday, someone has to bell the cat."* So pick your guts, and just do it.

40 The Law of Opposites

♠

A very old friend of mine claims to holds a patent on what he calls: "The law of opposites." ☺. He contests that the success rate of this law is more than 99%, provided the person on whom it is being applied has a working heart and an active brain!

He affirms, "The law always works. All you have to do is apply the opposite of what you face, and watch it in action.

I got to apply the same when my brother's only son was not treating him well. My brother was very old and lived with his son (quite common in Asian countries). But the treatment that he got from his son was very harsh. The situation became so bad that one day he rang up and asked me to register him in one of the old age homes. In his anguish he had called, as he simply wished to live peacefully for the rest of his life.

His plea angered me, and I decided to apply the law of opposites to get things straight. I called up my nephew and invited him to spend some time with me—to which he agreed. After a few days of his arrival, I took him to an orphanage under the pretext that as I was a trustee there, I needed to spend some time, reviewing their books. Once we reached there, I ensured that he had to spend some time with children of all age groups; while I reviewed their annual statements, and met the officials for my customary meetings.

To ensure that he did not run away I drove with him in my car, and kept the keys of the car with me! Finally, he was left with no choice but to be with the kids. He was thus *forced* to spend the whole day there.

On our way back, I told him, *'The kids loved spending time with you. You know why? Because they have never experienced how it feels to be with their mom or dad. They have never known how a father looks like or what a beautiful soul a mother is. Most of them were brought to this place when they were just few months old. They don't even know what a family looks like... So forget about any other relationship(s).*

We, as humans, never value what we get easily in life; and parents are something that we always take for granted, because they are the easiest 'things' that we could ask for. We always assume their presence to be our 'right,' and not a 'privilege,' that God has bestowed upon us—simply because we know they would stand for us, even when we do not ask for it. They would eat less to ensure that we sleep with our stomach full. They will make us wear good clothes, even if that means re-stitching the same patch of their own dress, year after year. And it is their graciousness that they will do all such acts wholeheartedly and happily, and not under any kind of obligation or pressure.

Parents rarely let go of their children, even when the going gets tough. But children let go of them, under the slightest of pressures. They move on...they move away. It is only when their own skin sags and bones weaken, they realize the gifts that their parents bestowed upon them. Now, look at yourself. You have already lost your mom and you are only left with your father to look after. While those kids had no control over their destiny, you, on the other hand, could still cover up. After all, the kids that you spent time with, never had a father like yours—who made his own life useless and meaningless, only to make your life meaningful and useful.'

By now, I knew the message had hit him hard, and I saw tears rolling down his cheeks. He stopped me and said, *'I have got the message. Please don't speak another word and take me back home.'*"

My friend continued with his narration as he shared another incident wherein he had applied his 'law.'

"And then there is another instance that I remember very well. There used to be a time when my son—in his teens—was addicted to video games. He used to spend hours and hours together with the same. So we thought of applying the law of opposites, instead of enforcing discipline. With his birthday round the corner, I declared, *'This time, we will celebrate your birthday with special people. It is a secret and you will come to know about it, only on your birthday.'*

On his birthday, me and my wife drove him down to a blind school with which we were associated. We spent the next 3-4 hours with the blind kids. We played games; made our son give away gifts and clothes to them; and had our lunch with them at their dining table. But throughout, we made our son to sit with them in the middle, while we took corner seats. The trip ended well and we drove back. As I glanced at my son in the rearview mirror, I saw him engrossed in his thoughts. When we reached home, he went to the mirror in his room and stared at his own image.

I noticed the same, went up to him and said gently, *'Son, one of the greatest gifts of God is a healthy body with perfectly functioning organs—be it our eyes, our hands, our legs, our ears or our nose. See how the world changes, when God snatches one of these vital parts of our body from us. You saw those kids, right? Ask them about their one wish in life which they want to come true, and they won't ask for money or fame. They would ask God to give them their eyes. Most of the time we don't treat our body with respect, and think of it as something which is to be taken for granted. The truth is, we need to respect our body first, before we respect anyone—and anything—else. Our eyes are precious. They are more precious than even the biggest diamond you could ever discover on this earth. Treat them well. The kids out there had no choice, but you have one. Make the right choices in life and use your eyes well. If you lose them once, you lose them forever.'*

Over the next few days I saw my son treating his body with more respect than I had imagined. He still played games, but within limits. As far as we were concerned, the law of opposites had helped us yet again.

Such instances occur frequently, just the context differs. Here is another one...

Recently, my young neighbor tried to commit suicide. I was stunned when I came to know of it. I saw an ambulance very early in the morning, as the siren woke me up. I rushed out, and saw doctors running out of the flat from the floor just below ours. I rushed down too. I knew the guy, lying on the stretcher in a pool of blood. His wife was crying uncontrollably and his 3-year old daughter clung to her mother tightly—too young to understand the drama that unfolded in front of her. All she could understand was that her daddy was not well. I accompanied him to the hospital, driving along all the way with the ambulance.

As I was driving, I recalled that he was a happy-go-lucky sort of a guy, in his early thirties. He was into stock-broking business and seemed to be doing pretty well in his life, as I always saw him driving the best cars and shopping at the most happening places. While he was being transferred to the intensive care unit, I noticed that he had slit the wrist of his right hand. I spoke to his wife, who was still crying. She told me about how they had lost a large part of their life's savings in one of the recent stock market fiascos. With the burden of a number of loans, the stress seemed to have overpowered his senses to ultimately result in a slit wrist. I knew some of the noted doctors in the hospital where he was being treated. I met them personally to ensure that he got the best possible treatment—not because I knew him very well, but his daughter's current state was too much for me to bear. And it is much harder, especially when you have a daughter back home who is almost of the same age.

A week later, I went to meet him and found him much better, and recuperating well. Doctors had allowed him to move within the hospital premises, in case he wished to stretch his legs. They had declared that he would be discharged from the hospital the next day. I went to my doctor friend and requested him to take both of us to the terminally-ill patients' ward. I knew it was tough for him to agree. I gave him another choice: to take us through the cancer patients' ward. He agreed, but under one condition: we would not utter a word or disturb anyone. I nodded. We then urged this guy to come out of his room on the pretext of a walk and passed through those wards...and he watched all those patients. On our return from this tour, I asked my doctor friend about some of those patients. He told us how they all were fighting internal battles with their bodies *every day*. Each one was a different story: if one was full of courage, the other exuded belief in God, while another one showed us how to fight smilingly. Yet, two things were common to all: pain and struggle...each day, each moment…for the rest of their lives.

After we were through with our discussion, I accompanied my neighbor back to his room. But by then, he was already engrossed in his thoughts, obviously affected by what he had seen few minutes ago. The time was just right for what I wanted to tell him. Taking the cue, I began...*'Do you know that most of the people whom you saw during your walk are going to die very soon? We all will die, but we don't know when. Hence, we spend our life almost casually. Imagine spending it, when you know you have only few weeks or few months to live. Now that will be tough, I tell you. That haunting thought will not even let you breathe peacefully, robbing you of life even when you are alive. All you will do is, count the rest of your days, without any objective or motive. You won't feel happy on meeting anyone. You won't enjoy food. In fact, you won't even feel like eating. You will reach a stage where life will look like a curse, with no signage for exit door. Yet, despite the perpetual trauma that they go through every day, they still fight to live, on the strong shoulders of hope and belief.*

On the contrary, look at yourself. You know what? You abused the gift of God--the gift of life...the gift of being alive...the gift of being healthy. On one hand, we have these people who know they won't live long, yet they fight hard to redeem their belief in God and respect the life that God has gifted them with. Ask them, about the true value of life—because life, like sand, is slipping away from their hands with each passing day. Learn from them. Just because you failed once in life does not mean that you start abusing it. When people like them can put up a brave fight every day, why can't you? So, no more of this stupid stuff in future. Now, take rest.'

Pouring out all that I wished to, I walked out of his room...and out of the hospital...leaving him with his thoughts.

The bottom line is: we need to be content with what we have—in the present—rather than worrying too much about the past or the future.

If you curse your 'old' car every day, go and use the public transport, only for a few days, to commute to your office. You will start loving it again, affirming: *old is gold*!

If you curse the public transport system for its ineffectiveness, then walk down to your destination for some days. You will suddenly start thanking the government for at least putting some basic infrastructure in place.

If you hate your toys, and curse your parents for not buying you the ones your friends flaunt every day, visit a nearby slum and see how kids play there. You will hug your old toys, the very next moment.

If you are unhappy with your promotion, simply because you did not get a good raise, meet someone who did not even a get a promotion.

You are not happy with your shoes? See someone walking barefoot.

You are not happy, walking barefoot? Watch someone walk with an artificial foot."

And I *have* to admit that I couldn't have asked for a better explanation and more appropriate examples—for the functioning and potency of the law of opposites. My friend has drilled its efficacy convincingly into my mind with utmost clarity.

41 The KYF Mantra

♣

Many times in life I have failed miserably. But each failure has led me to some profound learning, guiding me thus to a new meaning of failure.

I still remember one such incident wherein, my decision proved very costly for my company: it cost us a large project, which we lost and with it, lot of money. It goes without saying, the decision was taken after much deliberation and had been passed by my management. But what really haunted me was the fact: *I had pushed them into accepting my approach and thus, to the failure.* Even though my bosses told me to forget it as a one-off incident, it was extremely difficult for me to come out of the painful experience. Consumed by the pangs of guilt, very soon my self-confidence plunged to an all-time low. I started *going to* the management to *revalidate and confirm* each and every decision of mine, before taking the final call. I also became very hesitant in sharing my opinion during the brainstorming sessions. I found comfort and solace in silence, instead. I had suddenly become fearful of everything and hence, feared that my decisions would cause more harm to my company than good. I started believing that I was not fit for the role I had been entrusted with. The fear of failure loomed large all the time. The more I tried to come to terms with it the more I felt helpless.

Then one day, thankfully, I got a call from one of my mentors. It was a casual call. Since we had not chatted in the recent past, he had taken the initiative. Given our longstanding relationship, within minutes of our conversation he realized that something was amiss. When he probed further, I broke down and confessed how I had failed when my company banked on me to win. I admitted that I had been leading my life—since then—with the nagging fear of meeting failure again. When he heard everything, he smiled (*it was felt*) and then laughed (*which was heard*). I was taken by surprise with his response. I had expected him to sympathize and console me, and boost my sagging spirits. It being the contrary, I felt like putting down the phone.

As if he could sense my feelings, he started to speak just then... "You know what? If I were near you, I would have slapped you hard. This is the least I expected from a person of your caliber. How could you run away like this and be so afraid of making mistakes? This is not what I taught you when we worked together. Now grab a chair and sit down, because this call is going to last much longer than you can imagine." I followed his advice and made myself comfortable.

He continued, "Failures and mistakes are the key ingredients, of the wonderful 'dish' called happiness. Unless you fail, you will never be able to realize the true meaning of success, and you will never be able to measure the quality of your decisions. Remember, there is nothing called 'mistake,' in my life's dictionary. It is all about choosing between the bad, and the not-so-bad, that life has to offer. Yet, we are quick to label them as failures and successes in life. So don't be afraid of taking decisions. Fear can be constructive if you handle it well. Winston Churchill described success and failure as: *'Success is not final, and failure is not fatal; it is the courage to continue that counts.'* Do you agree?" I nodded in agreement. I was already feeling much better. For the past many weeks I had been tormented by this pain, and his words worked like a balm on them.

He went on... "Another quote that you must always remember in your life, is by David Neelman, Founder of the JetBlue Airways. He once said: *'What matters, isn't what happens to you in life; what really matters, is how you react to it.'* Do you now realize that you reacted very badly to whatever happened to you? Fear and failure are twin brothers, just like the brothers-in-arms. The only way to deal with them is to kiss one, and kick the other one."

Since I could not understand this logic, I interrupted him... "But what does that mean? I mean, the 'kiss and the kick' part. Please explain." Sensing my impatience, he responded, "Son, be patient. The next few minutes are going to be defining for your career and life. This you will realize when I explain what it all means. For the purpose, I present before you 'The KYF mantra.' Both sides of the yellow round-cut paper standee, which sits on my worktable, has KYF written on it. It serves as a constant reminder of this mantra's significance in my everyday life. The term KYF has two meanings. Hence, you have to view this standee as something which reflects two sides of the same coin—upholding two different perspectives of life.

The *first meaning* of the term KYF is: 'Kiss Your Failures.'

This will remind you of the fact that failures are very important in our life and hence, we must never shy away from them. When you encounter failures, just go ahead and kiss them. Because sooner or later, you will realize that these failures have actually helped you to become a better person in life. Finding it difficult to accept? Then let us play a memory game: close your eyes, and recall top five things that happened in your life in the last five years. Write them down on a piece of paper and then spend a few minutes, analyzing them. Go ahead... Do it now."

I immediately picked up a piece of paper and after thinking for a while, jotted down five things that came to my mind. When I was through with it, I reverted to my mentor.

He said, "Okay. Tell me what they are?"

And I complied obediently, "The first one is about a death in my family; second: the birth of my son; third: my last promotion; fourth: the failure as a friend, to one of my old college mates; and fifth: the incident we are discussing now."

"Did you notice that contrary to the popular belief—about how we love *only* the good things in our lives—your mind remembered one death, one new arrival, one success and two failures? Do we not wish this list to be full of *only* nice things, rather than deaths and failures? Still, you remembered your failures more than your successes. You know why? Because, the human brain is wired in such a way that it reacts more intensely to negative connotations and overtures that we face. And just because we remember our failures more than our successes, they are the ones which help us all along our lives—by acting as 'red zone' sensors.

Thus, they enable you to take better-informed decisions, compared to those in your previous encounters of the similar kind. They act like pathfinders, always showing you the right path—and like minesweepers, who would caution you on each step that you take in a corporate battlefield, with countless active minefields strewn all over the place."

With this, he took a small break and came back quickly, "I needed some caffeine badly. ☺. Coming back to our discussion, let me take a very simple example. One of my friends got divorced few years back. She was heart-broken, and labeled it as one of her biggest failures. But with time and little introspection, she recognized some of her own weaknesses, which she felt were responsible for her divorce. Since it was a bitter experience, it got imprinted on her mind, more than did anything else. So recently, when she started dating one of her office colleagues, her 'red zone' sensor worked more actively than ever before, reminding her what went right last time vis-à-vis what had gone wrong. It helped her take a more evolved decision this time. I am not saying that her decision, this time, would work for her. But I can surely say that her chances of making *this* relationship successful, is far more, compared to the earlier one."

"I hope this is making sense to you," he said and sipping his coffee, continued, "Human brain functions more intelligently when it encounters incidents of a particular nature. It is for the same reason that *my* way of judging people is very different from that of others. I judge them not by their experience, but by their incidents. Think about this proposition: you have an open position for a 'VP, Sales' in your company, and two equally experienced people apply. How do you know which one to select? The answer is simple: judge them on the basis of how they handled mistakes earlier in their lives. Chances are that one of them might have played safe in life. He might have run away from making those bold and risky moves and thus, would look impressive on paper and hence, an ideal choice. Contrary to this, the other one might have made mistakes, but had handled them well. You need to evaluate if he learnt from his mistakes and if he scored well in this area. If that be the case, you better close the deal with this person. *It is always better to choose the one who faced mistakes maturely, than the one who ran away from making them.* Because if your company faced the same kind of challenges in the future, and required someone to take those calculated risks for them, then, the one who had fled before, would still run away from it. But the one who has already handled such situations would handle it even more maturely this time, having learnt from his earlier failures under similar conditions."

By now, I was feeling much better and in fact, was enjoying our conversation.

So I asked eagerly, "Now what about the other side of the KYF- coin? What does *that* mean?"

He smiled and said, "I was coming to it. During this long journey of life, I have seen many people trying to run away from failures due to one simple reason: fear. I tell you dude, fear is the mother of all failures.

Therefore, the *second meaning* that I accord to the term KYF is: 'Kick Your Fears.'

Whenever you get into situations which make you fearful about the consequences, those are the ones which you need to fight fearlessly. Bring them down the *Real Steel* (the famous movie by Shawn Levy) way. Robin Sharma refers to this phenomenon as 'running towards your fear.' The life that we live every day is nothing but a game of choices that God wants us to play. We define our own life, based upon the choices that we make. If we make the right choices we are called Mr./Ms. Successful, and when we land with the wrong ones, we are labeled: Mr./Ms. Failure. To successfully overcome this dilemma—of choosing an option from the many that life offers—one should *not* to be fearful while evaluating them. It may sound simple as I speak, but believe me, most of us find it very difficult when it comes to the execution part.

I recently read a Harvard University research report, which described the effects of fear on the process of decision-making in humans. According to the report: when humans view anything through the lens of fear, the world appears to them as full of uncertainties—beyond their control, and rife with risk. While we are in the process of evaluating the available choices, our brain, which is wired to respond almost instantaneously to the negative parameters present in each situation, warns us against the negative consequences. This is when Mr. Fear gets a wild card entry. Once we get alarmed about the consequences, we become more cautious. It is at this point of time that Mr. Fear introduces us to Mr. Failure—and both of them, together, spin a hypothetical web inside our brain, forcing us to pick the choices which seemingly look harmless and safe. Sometimes, such choices do make us successful. But most of the times, they make us dumb. You may have heard the age-old saying about how practice makes the man perfect, right? So when you make too many safe choices, you become risk-averse and then you get into a vicious cycle. When you become risk-averse, you start opting for the safer choices with increasing frequency. This is exactly how *you* were functioning, when we started our conversation. You were deliberately making safer choices due to the fear of failure. Edgar Rice Burroughs said it so well when he observed: *'If I had followed my better judgment always, my life would have been a very dull one.'*" He laughed, and with him I laughed too.

"Now listen to this one... I heard in one of the recent movies that I saw, The Mechanic. The *hero* of the movie tells the guy, who was being trained by *him*, *'Good judgment comes from experience, and a lot of experience comes from bad judgment.'* Brilliant, isn't it?" he enquired, and continued to enlighten me further.

"So never be afraid of passing the wrong judgment or taking the bad decisions. Your decisions are the result of the choices that you make, depending upon your perception at that point of time. These define your true character as a person, in the long-term. In the corporate world, you tend to get attracted to a person who has done it and seen it all: the successes and the failures alike. Because deep inside your heart, you know that only such people can pull you out of the mess, in case you get into one some day. Why? Because they have gone through the same and handled it well in their past."

And thus he concluded, "Hey! I got to go to bed now. But I hope you got the essence of all that I shared. Correct? Always remember, life will throw choices at you all the time. First thing that you need to do is, evaluate those choices to the best of your knowledge. Of course, kick out Mr. Fear if he tries to barge in. *Once you have evaluated the choices that you have on the table, choose the one which makes absolute sense and then take the final decision.* If your decision backfires, do not get upset. Go ahead and kiss Mr. Failure. Thank him, as he just made you wiser and better prepared for the future."

As he concluded his counsel with these words, the fear and hesitancy that had weakened me from within left without any trace. I felt normal...my vibrant original self...again. I thanked my mentor for the same. After all, this is what mentors are for. You need them when the going gets tough. You need them, just as you need a straw when you are drowning. As the straw is big enough to hold on to and swim ashore, so are mentors— landing you safely on the shores of a meaningful life.

He signed off, with another quote to ponder upon, this time, one by **Martin Luther King**:

"Judge a man on how he reacts to failure, not success."

42 Finish your Meal

♦

"Finish your meal, otherwise I will not allow you to play outside. And yes, eat slowly and chew the food well." These are the directives that almost all mothers give to their kids repeatedly. And almost all kids (including my son, and me too when I was one) show their displeasure on hearing these words.

It is a very common sight at my home too! I have often seen my wife warning our son to finish his meals on time. I think she loves using these lines due to the following three reasons:

- She belongs to the species who ought to say it. ☺.
- The religion she belongs to does not allow one to waste anything.
- She feels that if we eat 'just right' and finish everything without wasting anything, it will *somehow*, *somewhere*, result in *someone* getting *some* food. She tells me, "If we stop wasting at the places where we eat, ordering only as much as we *can* eat, it will surely help in eradicating hunger from this planet—at least to some extent." Yet, despite her reiterations we often fail to implement it in our lives.

The underlying meaning of this line applies to many other domains, besides our lunch and dinner. As a metaphorical observation, it could simply mean: we must finish the task that we start. More often than not, I have come across many people who were brilliant all through—but only as planners of strategy or a project. They failed miserably, when it came to the implementation—and completion—of the very plan they themselves chalked out.

It seems they never listened to their mothers, in their childhood! In fact, it will not be an overstatement, if I tell you that such people—who can plan well, as well as implement their plans very well—have become rare in today's corporate world.

I remember my father as one such person who was very good at it, and I feel proud of having genetically inherited it from him. I recall how he would spend countless hours in fixing things at home (being an engineer, he loved doing things by himself and often taught us how to fix things quickly). Every Sunday, my mother would hand over a list of things to be fixed or completed, and he used to quietly spend hours completing them without any complaints. I also remember how every few minutes we would all try and pressurize him to complete it faster or leave it as such. But he would simply smile at us as he kept at it. He always took his own time to complete them to perfection, and his personal satisfaction.

He would simply say, "How you finish a job, says a lot about the kind of person you are in your real life." And I always used to shrug it off when I was young.

As I grew up and became more sensible, I came to know from his bosses and colleagues that he was an exact replica in his professional life too. He would spend hours, completing the tasks allocated to him. Since he was a 'bridge expert,' we used to accompany him to sites every now and then, so that we could play by the riverside. There, we would normally hear his friends and superiors talking highly about him. They would pat on our backs and tell us to be proud of belonging to his lineage.

I recall one of his bosses telling me once, when I was about to get into engineering college, "You must be proud of your dad because he always gives his best in whatever he does. He never screams or panics—no matter how tough the job is. Sometimes, he has to deal with the gun-toting, angry villagers who live by the ravines; and at times, he has to simplify the complexity involved in boring deep wells for the pillars of the bridge under construction. But I have never ever seen him fuss over anything. In fact, once I have assigned a task to him, I always know that he would come back only when it is finished. Moreover, he never believes in reminders. He completes each and every assignment on time, and with such great perfection and dexterity that you hardly find mistakes in his work."

During my graduation, when I started seeing the girl of my dreams (now my wife), I saw the same habit deeply embedded in her too. She used to be (*and is*) very detail-oriented, and always completed her assignments with perfection, even though she was one of the naughtiest in our batch. And now, I see our son too imbued with the same habit of completing tasks, no matter what comes in-between. (It is a different story that it is currently burning holes in my pockets and I will tell you how!) He is a voracious reader, and completes any new book so fast that I am forced to spend hours finding new ones, at the bookstores and at the airports. Similarly, whenever I buy him any new *Playstation* game, he plays it with great dedication and rests only when he has successfully cleared all the levels. I still remember buying him the famous: *The God of War* game. He came after a week and asked for the second game in the series. I was highly surprised to find that he had spent many hours, completing the first part to glory. Let us hope he extends the same habit to his studies, and later to his corporate life too. ☺.

After so many years that have passed, as I look back now, I feel so proud of picking this great habit from my father which, during those times, looked more like wastage of time. I have come across so many people in my life who would start new projects with great fanfare and enthusiasm, have fancy kick-off parties and get fully involved in the first few milestone meetings, only to find later that the initial steam had lost its strength midway, taking the project into 'the red,' be it through schedule slippage, effort variance or budget variance.

From a recent study by one of the leading IT research firms, I learnt that more than 65% of the projects in the IT world would either be stopped midway or took more time and money than was budgeted for them. And most of the time, you would notice that the enthusiasm around the project dies away somewhere along the line, without the team leader or the project manager even realizing it. *We need someone to act just like our mothers during such times and force us (with a perfect blend of love and little scolding) to finish the meal: the task at hand.*

I do remember how difficult it was to eat those last few pieces of bread. I would scream in protest, stating that my stomach was not able to take any more, while my mother knew that it could. She would divert my attention by telling stories, and put those last few pieces into my mouth. Similarly, when any project nears completion, we often notice that the team starts losing its steam, with the dampening belief that it cannot withstand the pressure anymore. Some of them would come and ask for a change of project, while others would start getting sick and take unplanned leaves—and some would simply run away.

Only a handful of dedicated team members remain till the end, being genuinely interested in completing the project and showing it the light of the day. Remember, how your mom used to handle those moments? She would sit with you at the table and tend to you lovingly; would talk to you about the things that mattered the most to you; and when you were very small, she herself would take those last few pieces and put them into your mouth. And before you could realize, the meal would be over and you would leave the dining table happily, and very much satisfied.

So all you have to do is apply the same lesson of life to such projects when they are nearing completion, and help them see the light of the day. Spend time with the teams and work it out with them; live the talk on the development floor and not in your cabins. Your teams need you the most when they are running low on batteries and thus, need to be recharged. They need you to speak to them about the good days that you spent together. *They need you to explain to them, why the completion of this project is going to be useful for them, for you and for the company that they work for.* They need you to instill that pride and honor, which comes as a bonus—when you see your project running into production and making lives easier for thousands of people around you. They need you to shower them with your love and affection, your support, your belief in them…and your assurance that everything will just be fine. Once you do that, you will see how your teams will re-gather their courage, re-focus their energies and work towards finishing the last pieces of their *meal.*

The following quote by **Zig Ziglar** holds the gist of this chapter:

> *"If you do the things you need to do, when you need to do them, then someday you can do the things you want to do, when you want to do them."*

43 You are the Boss!

♥

Do you still remember the tricks, teachers generally used to play on students during those good old school days?

Well, I hereby share, how it used to be with us. We had one of those typical naughty kids in the class who continuously troubled the teacher, no matter what. And then the teacher *had* to come up with his own trick to tackle the kid. He entrusted the kid with the responsibilities of a class monitor, thereby making the most undisciplined student accountable for the discipline of the entire class. ☺. This trick worked beautifully in those days. And it works very well even now, however surprising its still continuing efficacy might seem. It works wondrously, be it in the classroom of a school or the corporate world. Though nowadays, I have given this trick a new name: "You are the boss." The underlying principle remains the same, only reinforced by some additional twists. And the protagonist may not really be a naughty one or the troublemaker.

Let me explain the functionality of this trick in detail...

Sometimes, as a leader you get into situations where you need your direct line of reports, or your managers, to follow a certain decision. To do this two options are available to you. One is the to use of 'veto' power: simply implementing it at all levels. And the other option is to ensure that all have a proper understanding of the decision. Once that happens, you can push it down for acceptance, whereby an unanimous decision follows. While the first option is pretty straightforward to implement, our trick makes the second option easier to exercise.

An instance comes to my mind in this regard... There was a manager who was brilliant, yet very careless towards the 'quality processes' we used to follow in our projects. These processes were related to proper documentation and maintenance of other artifacts. And the reason for his carelessness was simple: he just did not believe in such processes. After trying hard, my seniors sought my help and *I knew it was time to play the trick*. I called a meeting with all my managers, under the pretext of giving them some general updates. Halfway into the meeting, I declared, "Guys, please welcome Mr. X (*honoring the privacy of the person, his name is not being used*) as the new 'process manager' of our business unit. He assumes his responsibilities with immediate effect, and he would spearhead the difficult task of ensuring that we follow all the processes within our projects. Along with, he will be responsible for the overall quality as well." The poor guy was left with his mouth agape. But with congratulations pouring in from fellow members, he thanked everyone and accepted the assignment gracefully. Little did he realize that in the process I had made him the 'class monitor.' Weeks later, when I checked on the progress, I was pleased to see that Mr. X had completed the task to perfection. At the same time, my purpose was served too: he understood the importance of these processes. Thereafter, I transferred him back to the role that he enjoyed playing. ☺.

There was yet another instance, when we were trying to push an important change at all levels. This change was related to the way we conducted the appraisals. As usual, we were using smooth and open communication as the medium to bring about the change. I came to know of a team leader who was apparently not happy with this change, and was spreading negativity around it. People who knew me, knew that he will soon be called up for a meeting...and that happened sooner than later.

My meeting ended within few minutes. I conveyed to him in a straightforward manner, "I have come to know that you are not very happy with the change we are trying to bring into this unit. And I am fine with that. I am even open to your suggestions, and the way you want this to be implemented. I will give you four weeks. Talk to your colleagues, and convince them for the way *you* want this to be implemented. If you succeed, I will go with you."

He sounded happy with my proposal and went away. Soon, four weeks went by, and there we were, facing each other again. He confessed, "In the last four weeks I have realized how difficult it is to implement a change; and even more difficult it is to implement the change by building a consensus around the same. I have now understood that every proposed change will always encounter opposition from a few people, and it is okay to have such situations. Over the last four weeks I have been spending so much of time—speaking to a number of people—about bringing this change in the way I wanted. It was tiring and yet, the result was not what I wanted. Now I realize, how difficult it must be for you to implement a change at all levels, keeping as many people happy as possible. I have learnt this the hard way and I apologize for the same."

My job was done. The trick had hit the target, right where I wanted it to. The intention was not to bring him down, but to make him realize: *many a times, it is not easy to keep everyone happy, and it is perfectly fine and natural if we find ourselves in such a situation.*

Most of the times I have seen folks not understanding how difficult things could be, because we have lost the habit of putting ourselves in the other person's shoes before jumping the guns.

One of my uncles told me once, "If you feel the pain yourself, then only you will understand how deep the wound is. Simply looking at the wound will not take you anywhere.

I have found most of the kids putting pressure on their parents to buy them symbols of their status, so that they can show them off in front of their peer group. This they do, as they don't realize how difficult it would be for those parents who are economically not *that* sound. I have seen some of the fathers even working overtime to make these useless ends meet and yet, they never seem to satisfy their ever demanding kids. I still remember that instance when my eldest son demanded more pocket money. His reason was simple: his friends were getting more than what he got and hence, it was becoming difficult for him to 'keep up' with them. Initially, I thought the demands were temporary. So I acceded to them, without thinking much about it. But soon, his demands kept on rising and that was when I decided to have an honest discussion with him.

I called him up and gave him a deal that he could not resist: for every 10 dollars that he earns by himself, I will pay him 20 dollars! But borrowing—from anyone—was not allowed. It had to be hard earned, and well-supported by checks and balances to testify the authenticity with respect to the conditions of the deal. Just within few days he realized my position and hence, stopped asking for more money. Rather, in the process he started respecting me more than before. Well, that was an added incentive and a pleasant surprise!"

What my uncle shared that day, is fully in accordance with what our sages have been stating since time immemorial: "A man realizes that *his* father was right only when *his* son tells *him* that *he* is wrong." And I fully agree with this time-tested observation.

44 Do you Treat them Royally?

♠

It was a bright Sunday morning. As I was going through the newspaper, searching for deals, I came across an advertisement. (And you thought deal-clinchers were found only in the corporate corridors!). It happened to be of the company whose broadband services I used. They were offering an extremely good deal on unlimited data usage plan. When I read further, I realized that I was paying more for the same data usage plan. Immediately I called their customer services department and requested them to change my plan to the one they had advertised in the newspaper.

To my surprise, the response that I got was: "Sorry sir. This plan is not for you."

Perplexed, I enquired, "What do you mean by that? You have featured a full page advertisement in today's newspaper, and I want *that* plan. Will you not be happy, to see a loyal customer of yours getting more perks with the same amount of money spent every month? Where is the issue?"

The executive replied, "Sorry sir. The plan, featured in today's newspaper, is applicable only to new customers."

By now, I was completely pissed off. I failed to fathom how could they offer something so lucrative, and still, keep it confined to only 'new connections?'

But I kept my cool and tried again, "Do you mean to say that the existing customers cannot use this plan?"

"Yes sir. Unfortunately, it is only for the new customers."

That went like the last nail in the coffin, and out came: "No problems. Please terminate my connection with immediate effect."

The customer care executive tried her best to pacify me, but failed.

I said, "Don't worry. I am going to re-apply as a *new customer*, with the *new plan* mentioned here."

With those words, I hung up.

Right through the entire day I felt very bad, having realized that such a reputed company had no respect for a 3-year old, loyal customer.

As if it was not enough, I encountered a similar incident after a couple of weeks. This time it was my bank, from whom I had taken a home loan. They were offering attractive rates of interest, but again, only for new customers applying for fresh loans. I visited the bank and requested them to convert my existing loan to the new rates. I got the same reply again... "Sorry sir. These rates are for new customers. We can't offer them to the existing customers."

When I argued, the bank manager called me into his cabin and said, "I can offer the new rates to you; but you will have to pay the conversion charges for that."

This seemed incredulous and I reacted, "You mean penalty charges!"

The manager was taken aback and confused, as was evident from his: "Pardon, sir?"

I stood by my conclusions and affirmed, "Of course! It indeed is a penalty that I must pay for choosing your bank."

I ended the conversation...and they lost an *existing* customer that very day.

While driving back home, I realized that nobody really cared about their existing customers. I could clearly see that their focus had largely shifted towards creating a new customer base, taking the existing ones for granted. The manner, in which even the bank manager dealt with me the other day, made it very clear that being an existing customer I was actually wasting his time (which, he seemed to be more interested in using for converting an existing one to a new prospect).

As an existing customer of many such services, I felt as if they did not need me anymore.

But I have always believed in loyalty-based membership cards. Because they not only give you a chance to earn reward points, but somewhere, deep within, I feel such companies do care for their existing customers. They want you to stay with them, even if that means parting away with some of their profits in the form of reward points.

Few days later I had a wonderful experience, which washed away all the negativities the two incidents—mentioned above—had imparted. In Hyderabad, on a business trip, I decided to catch up with one of my old buddies over dinner. After completing B.Tech he had decided to join his father's business and was doing fairly well. He invited me to his retail store in the evening as he wanted to show me his store. Since we had not met after graduation, so I hadn't seen his store too. Thereafter, we planned to go out for dinner together.

After finishing my task for the day at office, I headed straight to the address—of his store—that he had given to me. He was running a gift shop, fairly large and very popular too. I became aware of its popularity because the taxi driver straightaway took me to the place, as soon as I told him the name of the same. On reaching the store, my friend greeted me and gave a tour of the store.

One of the particular sections in his store caught my attention. It was the one with the hanging placard: "Loyalty pays." Since I was badly hit on account of loyalty—during the past few weeks—curiosity killed the cat, and I asked him, "Hey man! Tell me more about this one."

And he complied, "The items in this section are priced at heavy discounts—but, available only for my loyal customers. They can buy any one item from this section at heavy discount, on their each visit to the store." I was impressed and urged, "Please continue."

And he did...

"See buddy, I am a very small businessman. I can't afford

to spend large amount of money on advertising and publicity. *The only way I can advertise is* by piggybacking on my existing customer base, and making *them* talk about my store within their friend circles. Which is why I ensure that I treat my customers royally. They have to feel special every time they shop here. Irrespective of whether they shop for a few items or make large purchases, I do not discriminate when it comes to their loyalty. They are all treated with equal respect: as kings and queens."

The conversation became interesting. On one hand, I had experiences with companies (1000 times larger than his store) who were not even thinking about loyalty, leave aside treating the loyal customers royally, they being more interested in the inorganic growth. On the other hand, I was listening to this small-time businessman, who was trying to make a difference by treating his customers royally.

Meanwhile, my friend continued, "I have even kept the process of 'loyalty rewards' very simple. I use their cell numbers as my primary identification key. The system I have designed has three tiers of loyalty, based on their annual spending with us. They don't have to carry any membership card. Some of them do not even know that they are a member of my loyalty program and belong to one of the tiers within the same. Everything works in the background. We track the customer's spending, and the system upgrades them automatically. There are times when we surprise our customers by offering them any product—of their choice—from the "Loyalty pays" section at great discounts. And you know what? Words cannot describe the pleasant surprise that reflects on their face during those moments. It is an immeasurable experience, as an owner of the store. They feel so elated when they get such a princely treatment, and that is very much evident from their expressions. We also offer value-added services corresponding to the tier of their membership—again, all is evaluated in the background, based on their spending with us. We offer discounts during the billing process, and *surprise* the customer with such *sweet shocks*. Sometimes, after the billing is complete the sales executive would hand over free coffee coupons, which can be used in the small in-store cafeteria. *The key to success here is the surprise factor. You need to surprise them and make them feel special.* They need to feel that we care for their repeated visits to the store and, are very thankful to each one of them. The only way to reciprocate their loyalty is by way of these small gestures. Come this way, I will treat you to a taste of coffee at my coffee shop."

A minute later, we were in the coffee shop, enjoying some good South Indian coffee. Taking a sip, he continued, "In order to ensure that we do such things as a team, it is very important for my staff to understand the culture that needs to percolate at all levels. Therefore, while we treat our customers royally, we also treat our ground staff in a similar fashion: they too get rewarded, in keeping with their behavior. *The rule is plain and simple: make the shopping experience as painless as possible for the customers. At the same time, the ground staff is instructed not to disturb them, unless called upon.* The customers have to experience their shopping with us.

And then we have a 'return policy' as well. Unlike many stores, where they do honor 'returns' but with caveat, which could be: *'No returns on weekends and Sundays'* (which is when most of the people go out and complete their weekly chores) or restrict the timings between 1 p.m.-4 p.m. (again, when nobody can come out of their offices for a damn return). Contrary to this, we have a straightforward policy: *'Return any day, any time, within 15 days of the purchase.'* No questions are asked. Sometimes, we have even gone overboard—for some very loyal and high-tiered customers—when we accepted the 'returns' even *without* receipts. All in all, everything in my store depends upon their loyalty and spending with us. Another coffee?"

I replied, "Sure, the coffee is real good."

We continued with our discussion. By now, I was feeling very proud of my friend. And he kept on enhancing this feeling as he continued... "Can you guess, where did I pick all this? Okay, let me take you back in time when I joined my father's business. At that time, we used to buy many items from one of my father's loyal suppliers. He was not educated, but knew how to handle his customers well. His relationship with my father began years ago, and they were very happy dealing with each other due to the trust that got built between them over the years. When I took over, he came and met me. During the next few years, I realized that though the market was getting costlier, the rates at which this supplier gave us the material were much cheaper than what others offered. So one day, I went ahead and asked him the reason behind the same. It was then that he shared his secret and out came the word: 'loyalty.' I was so surprised when I heard all about it. He was supplying the goods to us at a very attractive rate and was making lower margins while dealing with us. His reasoning was two-fold:

- He acknowledged that he made money from many new customers, which he made each day—courtesy, my father, who was his biggest word-of-mouth publicist.
- Such a trick made him survive the difficult days of recession. Thanks to his loyal customers, like my father, who continued to buy materials from him even during downturns and thus, kept him afloat in the market. He loved his customers so much that they too chose to stick with him through ups and downs in his business.

That day, I realized that basically you need common sense and nothing else, to run your business. When an uneducated supplier like him could be so street-smart while dealing with his customers, why couldn't I? Since then, I have been following his 'principle of loyalty' while running my business. ☺."

Overwhelmed by this entire discussion, we hugged each other and headed straight for our dinner. While driving to the venue, I introspected...

> All those big talks around organic vis-à-vis inorganic growth have been blown out of proportion. Companies spend a bomb over creating a brand for themselves. Yet, miss out on their existing customers and their loyalty so

easily. If they could spend half of their time and energy, worrying about their existing customers, they would achieve so much more with the same dollar spent. After all, it is all about common sense—pertaining to how you treat your existing customers.

45 Last Mile Connectivity

♣

Recently, one of my my wife's cousins visited us. He was studying in one of the reputed engineering colleges in India, and was in Delhi for his first summer training. He had joined a telecom firm and was entrusted a project related to 'last mile connectivity.' With him I relived my engineering days and we had some great discussions around the topic over tea and biscuits.

People working in the telecommunications domain might very well relate with the term: 'last mile connectivity' and the challenges associated with it. But for those who are not aware of this term, here is what *Investopedia* says: *"A phrase used in the telecommunications industry to describe the technologies and processes used to connect the end customer to a communications network. The last mile is often stated in terms of the 'last mile problem,' because the end link—between consumers and connectivity—has proved to be disproportionately expensive to solve."*

Furthermore, if you look up the term in *Wikipedia*, you will find that they add another beautiful line to the definition above: *"Because the last mile of a network, to the user, is also the first mile from the user to the world—with regards to sending data (such as uploading)—the term 'first mile' is sometimes used in conjunction."*

After he went back, I plunged deep into thoughts relating to this topic. I realized that an analogy could be drawn between this deep-rooted problem in the telecom domain and a typical corporate organizational structure.

To me, 'the last mile connectivity' is nothing but 'the last man connectivity': a problem that exists in almost each and every organization that we could think of. And worst, we are hardly aware of its existence.

How many times have we *really* worried about the bottom-end of our organizational pyramid and thought about their issues, concerns and welfare? How many times have we really walked across the floor and listened to the issues that our junior most staff faces every day? Those issues could be petty, but are we hearing them out? As decision-makers for our organizations, we have become so busy, fighting battles in the boardrooms, that we have lost out completely on the 'last man connectivity' factor.

We simply cannot avoid this fact. We can defend ourselves and spend hours, explaining: how our organization is structured; how we ensure that communication flows in all directions; how we have implemented an honest open-door policy (*which is hardly open-door in reality, except that we keep our cabin doors open to let the fresh air in*)...and the like, as many more explanations and clarifications are forwarded.

Quite often, we have failed to realize that the strategies and vision, which we create for the organization, are like a dead fish. It breathes life only when the people—right at the bottom of the pyramid—get connected to them, and start working towards manifesting them. Picking a leaf from the life of Steve Jobs, yet again, I found out that he was not just good but one of the best—in successfully handling the issues related to the 'last man connectivity.' He used to connect with people at all levels by walking up to them and discussing things in the open. And the enthusiasm and connection, which was so apparent in the people working at Apple, reflected in the passion with which they created and sold their products. Since the employees of Apple felt connected to their leader, they made his dreams a part of their own dreams. That is how you solve this problem.

Let me explain why it is so important for *all of us* to solve this problem of 'last man (mile) connectivity.' The 'last mile connectivity' issue is sometimes also referred to as the 'first mile' problem. First mile, because that is how you get connected to the outer world.

Picture these for a moment...

- *How many times have you walked out of a potential purchase, simply because you did not get the right kind of attention from the sales executive at the shopping mall?*
- *How many times were you frustrated because you didn't get a proper response to your insurance-related queries over the phone?*
- *How many times you walked into an automobile showroom but returned, utterly confused, because the executive could not explain the features of your dream car properly?*
- *How many times did you avoid staying at the same chain of hotels, just because they spoiled your last vacation with their sloppy service?*

Given the experiences that we have in general, I think your answer in all probability will be, "Such instances have been many." Do you think it is the quality of the products that are responsible for your experiences? No. It is not the products, but the company's 'first mile' employees who spoiled the game. Even if you have the best products or services to offer to your customers, these do not really count, unless the people who are responsible for connecting the customers to you are passionate about them. It is not only *what* you offer that is important, but *how* you offer it is equally important.

All you need to do is carry a spot check:

- To see if your own employees—who face the customers—are passionate enough to serve them well, with the requisite dedication for what I call 'customer's delight.'
- Whether they are enthusiastic about the work they do.
- Are they really excited to work for your company?
- Do they connect with the goals and vision of your company? Because if they are not connected, very soon your *customers* will disconnect *themselves*—from your products and services.

The only way to overcome this challenge is by keeping the

connection between you and your employees alive. If you are well-connected at all levels within your organization, you ensure that they understand and hence carry your vision and objectives well. At the same time, it also enables you to uproot bad practices prevalent in your teams much before they become tumors for you. It is always advisable to remove fibroids early in the cycle before they become dangerous. For that, they need to be detected well 'in time.' And the ways to find them out 'in time': self-evaluation of your body and regular check-ups at the clinic. In corporate parlance, self-evaluation in this context simply means: being connected with all parts of your organization.

It reminds me of one of the CEOs who was brilliant at staying connected at all levels. Very often, he would take office transportation and mingle with employees at all levels, without letting them know who he was. He had that incredible quality of mixing with employees of any age group. This enabled him to learn about the issues and the areas of concern straight from the horse's mouth.

He once told me, "Most of the people rely on just one form of communication—the one that flows from their direct reports to them. What if their 'direct line' of managers painted a rosy picture in front of them? You have no way of verifying what is actually happening on the ground, unless you walk the floor yourself. If an employee has complained about the bad quality of microwaves installed in the cafeteria, you better go down and heat your pizza there once. Because the microwave installed for the top management's use would never go out of order. So, unless and until you go down and test a microwave yourself, the picture would always appear rosy.

There was once an employee who wrote to me while working at a client's site. His issue was related to the daily allowance that he was provided. He sent me detailed calculations on how the client's city proved to be costly enough to question the allowance that he was allocated for the upkeep of his family. When I went to my 'direct line managers,' they told me that everything was fine and the employee was being unreasonable with his demands. Somehow, I could not believe them fully. Hence, I told one of my trusted guys to fly down to the city and spend a week, in order to understand the problems on the ground and report back. And he returned with lot of surprises. The city had indeed proved to be too expensive to sustain a living with the allowance that we were providing. Worse, it had a negative psychological impact on the employee, and this reflected on his productivity levels. When you are not happy from within, it affects your mind too and that can be sensed easily by your customers. So, while it may look like an employee's issue, it is actually you who should be more worried, because it tells on the quality of service provided to your customers. Do not forget: if you are well-connected with your employee base, then in reality, you are well-connected with your customers too."

And again we refer to Steve, in this context as well, because he was very particular about the people—in totality—who were employed at the Apple stores: their dress, their behavior, their etiquette, and their passion and love for the products that they were entrusted to sell. He always believed that if his people on the floor loved their iPods and iPads—to the extent of considering them as their second skin—they would be able to passionately explain (the salient features), and sell the same to the prospective customers.

Another person, to whom I can relate in the context of this 'passion principle,' is **Jack Welch**. In one of his books he explained the '4 E' and '1 P' framework, which he implemented across General Electric (GE) during his tenure as the CEO. The framework was implemented during their hiring process. The '4 Es' stood for: positive energy, ability to energize others, edge (ability to take tough decisions) and execute (ability to finish tasks). Only after any candidate had passed the '4 Es' he/she was evaluated for 'P,' which stood for passion. Jack believed in passionate people.

In his own words: ***"The funny thing about passionate people is that they usually aren't excited just about work. They tend to be passionate about everything. They are sports trivia nuts or they are political junkies. Whatever—they just have juice for life in their veins."***

So stand up, and move out of your cabins. Meet the 'last man standing,' and show him that you care. Hear him out. Make him feel special. Make him experience the passion that *you* bring on the table, every day, and get him connected—rather, addicted—to it. After all, it will be prudent on your part, not to make the 'last man connectivity' issue, the 'first customer connectivity' issue for your organization.

46 Let us Un-complicate

♦

It was quite late when our house phone rang one night. We became apprehensive of some bad news, and I hurriedly went ahead to answer the call. On the other end of the line was a female voice—hardly understandable and crying uncontrollably, she asked for my wife. I was kind of surprised to hear someone asking for my wife, and that too, so late into the night. Since me and my wife had graduated from the same college, most of our friends were common. But I could not recognize *her* voice and hence, handed over the phone to my wife without any ado. She spoke for a while and then commanded, "I am not listening to you anymore. Take the next available flight and come here. We will sort it out together." When she had hung up, I asked who the caller was. I was taken aback when I heard her name—she was one of the best friends of my wife, and seemed to be going through a rough patch in her marriage.

Very soon, she paid us a visit. Over the next few days we spent a lot of time, trying to understand what had gone wrong. More so, because she herself had chosen her partner. And for that very reason she was hesitant to go back to her parents and share her current state of affairs. We promised to help her, and she in turn assured that she would honor our recommendations—even if that meant retracting few steps in certain areas. The only saving grace was her intention to save the marriage. Meanwhile, we thought it would be a good idea to call her spouse as well to spend some time with us. Christmas had approached by then. Since we had already applied for a week-long vacation, taking the time out—to settle their matter—fitted well in our scheme of things.

After many rounds of discussions we arrived at the following conclusions.

1. She cited various instances, for which we blamed lack of communication, as it led to the misunderstandings that had started creeping between them. Both had bright careers and were spending too much time in the office, rather than with each other. Even on weekends, one of them invariably would be at the airport—courtesy, official trips—while the other one would be busy spending time with friends. Hence, we recommended:

    - They must stay together during weekends, to start with.
    - It was imperative for them to take some time out for at least one vacation every quarter.

    We reminded them of those times when they romanced each other during our college days. They used to sit together for the classes; would hangout together in the cafeteria; and spent most of their time chatting with each other.

    This is what I told them...

    "What happened to that die-hard romance, which was written all over your faces during your undergraduate years? Why do we change priorities, when we get married or get into high profile jobs? I can see that soon after marriage you started taking each other for granted, and assumed everything to be perfectly normal and fine, while it was not. You stopped spending time together, because you wanted to buy a home, a flashy car and lots of diamonds. For what? Now that you have all the money to spend, do you think it is helping you to save your marriage? You remember, how we used to give roses to our sweethearts on Valentine's Day? The institution of marriage is also like a red rose plant. In order to keep its roses fresh, you need to sprinkle water daily. The day you forget to water the plant, you will notice it drooping down. Even if you make millions on that day, you still cannot save the rose plant from dying—because it needs water, and not money, to survive and flourish. If you can use money as a 'manure for the rose plant,' rather than substituting it for water, only then your hard earned riches will bring you joy and happiness in life."

They needed to understand that for relations to blossom (whether personal or professional), the communication has to be very frequent, honest and open. And by communication, I mean face-to-face and not the one via: cell phone, e-mail and chat. Somehow, with the technology giving us more avenues to be in touch, in reality it has drifted us apart. I know of a couple, who converse mostly using 'electronic chat' during their office hours. I asked them why and they replied, "We simply don't get the time." One of them is always on the road... At the same time, communication is effective only when it comes with a personal touch. Communicating, simply for the sake of it, serves no purpose. Another friend of mine has this habit of taking his wife out for lunch on weekdays. He does it once or twice a month and acknowledges that they tend to be very effective in maintaining the freshness of their relation in the long-term.

2. Second thing that we noticed was the ego factor. We found out that on the many occasions they fought, they were not ready to patch-up, simply because they expected the other person to make the first move. More often than not, I have realized that ego could be the mother of all personal and professional issues that we face. In fact, each and every dispute—that I have resolved within my teams—had ego as the root cause. While we all know how damaging our egos could be, yet we always succumb to it.

And it is affecting the younger crowd more, where the patience levels are going down faster than the rising hemlines. A small argument...and it turns into an ego fist-fight. The master strategist, Kautilya, observed brilliantly in the context of managing relationships: "One who gains upper hand in a relationship—or decision—need not always be the one who wins the battle. Sometimes, victory is achieved by going on back-foot."

Coming back to this couple under consideration, we cited such examples to them where ego had disastrously ruined marriages—and in some cases, how it had even led the couples to go as far as filing nasty divorce suits which, before they could even realize, was too late for either of them to retract.

Then my wife took over and explained further...

"Let us go back to the college days once again. Do you think anyone of you really cared about who won those small fights that you used to pick up? In fact, to be honest, deep inside your heart you always wanted the other person to win the argument, even though you knew that you were right and the other person was wrong. Because, then you had not allowed your egos to take decisions on your behalf. Matters of the heart are solved best when they are left to the heart, and not entrusted to the mind. Mind is where the ego resides, while heart is where your selfless love resides. Then how come over the years you allowed ego and love to swap their homes?

Tell me one thing: have you ever filled credit card or bank account forms? There are two sections for mentioning the addresses. One is for your 'present' address, while the other is for your 'permanent' one. While your present address can change, depending upon the prevalent conditions, the permanent address remains true to its meaning, i.e., permanent. Similarly, love and romance has to reside in the permanent address column, within your hearts, and not in the column for present address: your mind. If you can somehow keep a constant tab on this parameter throughout your life, you will always remain blissfully happy in this beautiful relationship called marriage. And once you ensure that 'love' resides in the permanent 'heart' address permanently, then even if ego creeps into your present address, anytime during your life, you will still be able to deal with it and kick it out. Remember, home is where your permanent address is!"

3. The third reason behind their strife was the feeling of a loss of identity, in trying to please the partner. Both of them belonged to different religions, and in order to please their respective families they had resorted to temporary compromises. Very often, people behave or live in a manner that tends to shadow their original personality. I call it a short-term strategy, which can work, but only for a while. From a long-term perspective, it is definitely going to fall flat. I remember one of my uncles advising me with some powerful lines of wisdom on the occasion of his silver wedding anniversary: "If you live with an identity which is not yours, things are bound to go wrong after it reaches its tipping point. You can't live a superficial life for long—just like water, which will always find its natural path. Imagine your relationship to be like a rubber band. You can keep on stretching it, but only till a certain point, after which one of the two things would occur: either it snaps, or if you release it, it comes back to its original shape—but not without hurting the person holding that end of it. So the bottom line is: any relationship cannot survive for long if we don't know how to respect and accept the other person in his/her natural form."

   Having recalled my uncle's advise, I explained the same to them...

   "Any relationship, built on mistrust and compromises, will never survive—no matter how hard you try. Marriage has to be viewed as an extreme form of friendship; a friendship, which is as pure and gentle as glycerin. As in true friendship, which is unconditional, you must never

> expect the other person to change his/her behavior for the survival of your marriage. Because survival is an extreme form of compromise...and compromises never work in marriages. Unless both of you work together, as two dots trying to form a line, you will never be able to form one. It has to be a two-way process. So even if you have to please your respective families, do it as a line and not as dots. Remember: dots when placed in silos, have no meaning. Priority is another aspect that needs to be catered to. While pleasing your families, the priority should be to maintain your love and face it together, rather than it being the other way round. The idea is to cover each other up as a team and create a protective shield which saves both of you—from the harmful radiations emitted by such circumstances."

During those two weeks, we could notice things getting back to normal between them. Both me and my wife were very happy to have utilized our vacation in saving someone's love life. My wife rejoiced on seeing her friend back in her natural form, and thanked his spouse for enabling their relationship to survive through this bad phase. Bumpy roads would always be there. But they do not matter as long as we drive carefully, avoiding the pitfalls in the process.

As we bade them goodbye at the airport, I remembered what **Zig Ziglar** has written in one of his books:

> ***"How many marriages would be better if the husband and the wife clearly understood that they are on the same side."***

P.S. For my international readers, I share an information which they might not be able to access otherwise. It concerns the title of the chapter and the inspiration behind the same. "Let's Uncomplicate" is the brilliant tag-line used by a leading health insurer in India, in a very famous advertising campaign of theirs.

47 Everyone is in Sales

♥

This incident dates back to the time when I used to work for a 'startup' company. Those were the years of global dotcom boom. I was one of the main guys in the startup, and our company had developed a 'learning management system' (LMS). We were looking to generate revenue via two routes: by licensing the LMS, and by running it as a service—tying up with some leading content providers, famous universities and training companies.

During one of the trade seminars that I attended, I met a person from a company which dealt with DVD-based training material. His company was looking for a platform to host the same on the internet. That was more than what I could have asked for, as I was looking for the content to be hosted using our software. Hence, it was a perfect handshake. Naturally, I invited him to our office to chart out some intricacies around partnering, and plan a 'go to market' (GTM) strategy together.

One fine morning, he came with a team of three people to our office. We had already exchanged our visiting cards at the seminar. As his card read: 'VP, Sales,' I knew he was from the sales department. When I greeted his first teammate, he bowed and gave his card and it too read: 'VP, Sales.' I was surprised. But then I thought: they might be having two of them, to cover the whole of India under two regions. I moved over to his second teammate, and this time my surprise knew no bounds as his card also read the same! By the time I reached his third teammate, I had guessed his designation...and it was proved right. Thus, for the first time in my life, I was in a room with four people from a small company—and all of them were 'VP, Sales!' It looked like an adventure of a lifetime was in the offing.

As the reason was hard to fathom, before getting into the agenda of the meeting I honestly conveyed, "Guys, before we start you need to kill my curiosity. How do you manage four people with the same designation, for a startup like ours?"

The one with whom I was already acquainted, smiled. He waved his hands, pointing to—and encircling—all of his colleagues, and replied, "Everyone is in sales!"

Seeing our blank faces, he continued, "The one on my right, takes care of human resources. His job is to sell our company's uniqueness to prospective employees and thus, help attract the best talent, which would otherwise be very difficult for a small startup like ours. We go to the best colleges each year, and this man does a great job: selling the idea of joining our company, to young brains. While we do not pay more than what the market has to offer, he has built a unique salary structure, which would look attractive even to the minds of people like us. So it goes without saying that the young kids get attracted to his ideas, just like a bear is to honey. Back home, he keeps reaffirming the company's salient features to every employee, so that we do not lose them to competition. We invest heavily in training our staff, and this guy ensures that only we get benefited, and not our competitors.

The one to my left, takes care of our finances. His job is to sell our strong and accurate financials to all the 'venture capital firms' who invest in our company. With the great job that he does at selling 'numbers,' he ensures that we keep getting the desired funding from our parents (read: those who invested in our company), when we need it the most. What we have learnt over the years is that the CFO (read: chief financial officer) has to be a master sales person, for companies of our size to survive the heat of competition and demands of the stakeholders. These days the stakeholders have become ruthless. They want results even faster than you could expect your ideas to be accepted in the target market arena. If your CFO can crunch numbers in such a way that the forecast looks great to the shareholders, then you are saved—otherwise you are a dead fish."

And then he went ahead to introduce the last guy... "The one who is in the front, manages the delivery and development of the products that we market. His job is to develop the content we create—in the most creative of ways—for our clientele and thus, ensure that they get the finest quality of products delivered to them. He is responsible for the high customer satisfaction we achieve in the process. It is because of him that we enjoy the loyalty of our clients. He is the one facilitating the free word-of-mouth publicity from our clients—who refer us to other prospective clients interested in similar services. He is the one who puts our company's products and services in front of our customers. So when it comes to explaining our products and their detailed features, he does a great job at selling those to new and potential customers. Over the years, we have learnt that building a great product and explaining its features are two different ball games, and this gentleman is great at both of them. The person explaining the features must have awesome communication and presentation skills. He must be imbued with an ability to weave an interesting story around our products in such a way that it becomes a cake-walk to convert that prospect into a reality. And that is what this man catalyzes."

On hearing this, I was not only impressed but was deeply touched as well. The way the four of them operated as a team was truly commendable.

He concluded by saying, "Each one of us has to wear our sales hat at all times—be it our deliverables or our financial scorecard or our credentials—to attract the right talent and client. If we don't do it, we will surely be out of business. And by the way, I am the 'Real Sales' guy, whose job is to sell our company's products. Herein, I have to admit that these three gentlemen make my life very easy and charming."

The meeting went well, and we worked as partners till the time I made a job switch. All four of them have joined different companies now, but are doing very well in their respective fields—and I know the reason behind their success. ☺.

Years have passed by, but as I have remembered this principle so I try my level best to implement the same—wherever and whenever my life gives me an opportunity to do so.

And one such opportunity I had when I was entrusted with the entire responsibility (development and services) of one of the products that was being launched by my company. It was developed using a proprietary language. The product was great, but there was a 'catch' (read: challenge) involved. Anyone who joined this product's team would have to undergo training on this language, which was not at all a cool thing—especially in the IT world, where the more high-end are technologies that you work for the higher your 'hip quotient' goes.

The only saving grace till then was that the product sold very less. So we always managed with a small team somehow. But then there came a month in which we saw sudden increase in demand for the services of this product. This meant: we had to ramp-up quickly to meet the demands of our customers and along with, grow this business, which had been dormant for so long. So I pulled out people from my other teams and asked them to meet the guy, who according to me, had the competence for the purpose (and hence, I made him the product manager). I sent several people to him over the next few weeks, to ensure that we could start the training at one go. But to my surprise, people kept coming back to me with different excuses, stating thus their inability to join this guy's team.

Out of those excuses some where outright lame...

Some of them said, "The technology is too old and I don't want to stick with something which has no market value." A few declared, "Documentation is deficient. I don't think I will be able to learn this so quickly." While some others were blunt enough to state, "I am happy where I am. If you move me to this old generation product, I will quit."

Surprised by such responses, I decided to meet some of them for a detailed discussion and find out the truth... And then I found what the actual issue was. It pertained to the product manager himself. Though he was great at this alien language, he was poor at selling it. So, all those who met him, came up with frightful responses. He made two mistakes: he gave longer and more detailed answers than was required of him; and he could not sell the uniqueness of the product convincingly to these folks. He failed to realize that even for attracting talent within the company, we must be artful at selling the salient points of the project on which they would get the opportunity to work. At the same time, we should be able to highlight the short-term and the long-term rewards, that come along with as bonus.

Once I became aware of the actual scenario, I called him and said, "You are in sales, buddy! So wear that hat before you meet the next person." I taught him how to sell his product(s) to the customers—and the project to his staff. And that included emphasizing upon *one of most significant attributes* of the project: *working for such a niche area would never render them jobless—not even during the scariest of the recession periods*. I spent time with him and a couple of potential team members, to demonstrate how to sell products and attract people to join his group. He was brilliant and picked up the clues. And now his group has some of the brightest people—highly motivated by the technology, which is as old as my great granddad. ☺.

Similarly, when I have to hire for some key positions within my business unit, I take charge of it. The reason: you need to sell your group's USP to the candidates in the best possible manner, so as to attract the finest talent available. Just as much as *they* need you, *you too* need the best talent to work for you. While the initial reason behind posting a resume to your company's website, is its brand, their decision to join your company depends on how well you sell your work and projects to them. Come to think of it, Steve Jobs used to hire all his key people himself. He was a master at selling dreams to all: whether they were his customers, his employees, his shareholders or his board members. He was just awesome and we all need to learn from him, *all the time*.

If you have read Lee Iacocca, you will know that he was hell of a master salesman himself. When Steve Jobs wanted to meet him for the very first time, Lee agreed, but on one condition: he wanted Apple to hire Chrysler's (Lee was its chairman then) Dodge Caravans! No wonder, companies with such great, focused leaders have always done well at the marketplace—without having to worry at all about economy and recession.

Till date, I have never forgotten this golden rule: "Remember, we are all in sales!" I share this with the fresh campus graduates, and keep reiterating it to all members of my staff.

48 Over-speeding Thrills, but Kills

♠

I love my country unconditionally, even though there are moments when I really get upset about certain things that I face. One of them is the erratic driving by the people in Delhi. Over the years, the Delhi government has tried hard to control and curb rash driving and out of the many ways that they have adopted, one is the putting up of billboards—every few hundred meters—which speak about the potential hazards of dangerous driving. The most commonly seen is the one which declares: "Over-speeding thrills but kills."

While commuting to the office I see this billboard at an intersection. And every time I see it, I reminisce on the *two* human qualities, which if not controlled, can be fatal. However, I must confess: both of these qualities *do* cause adrenaline rush, providing the same kind of kick that is derived while driving fast.

The *first* one is our **ambition.**

It is one of those rare medicines available to human beings, which when consumed in rightly administered doses, can work wonders—and if gorged on, uncontrolled, can prove to be disastrous.

Each year, I come across very sharp individuals, with all the passion and energy to make a difference in the corporate world. Some of them are so ambitious that they focus solely on getting things done, and direct their energy in accordance. They are least bothered about 'how' they accomplish it. Yet this is what separates the men from the boys.

Let me cite some examples, which would answer why it is very important to pay attention to 'how' a thing is done. To me, feeding your ambitions is futile, if you miss out on all those great moments in life that involve your family and friends. It is similar to driving at such a speed that you don't even realize the presence of your partner, sitting next to you. Our focus being on the steering and the speed, the pleasure associated with a long drive is lost on us. The same rule applies to those who stab others to fulfill their own ambitions. They race ahead of others by overtaking from the 'wrong side' of the driving lane. But I don't blame them at all. It is their ambition that is to blamed. Their ambitions are absolutely untamed, as their mind is fully controlled and driven by the kick of their ambition. End result: they might be successful in the short run, but in the long run, trust me, they are the biggest losers. *Just like the 'tickets' you get for your reckless driving—and are penalized—you get similar tickets in your real life too.* They could be in the form of losing your family, friends, relations… It could be anything...

And then there are others who burn themselves out in the heat of their ambitions. I have come across many such people who worked like hell for the major part of their young age, only to become fully exhausted and saturated pretty fast. *Talking about their share of tickets, they lose out on their health and start living their life out of a prescription*. Is that what they had striven for? Is that what they earned those dollars for…to spend it later...on their visits to the hospital, meeting doctors and buying medicines? If yes, then God bless them!

However, if your ambition is controlled just like driving a car at a reasonable speed, then you not only reach your destination safely, but actually enjoy the drive and the journey associated with it. And not to forget: in a country obsessed with mileage, you get bonus in the form of better fuel efficiency—derived from your same car and same life!

Even the laws of nature support this theory. I recently read the great book by *Dr. Siddhartha Mukherjee*, a Pulitzer prize winner in the non-fiction category, *Emperor of all Maladies: Biography of Cancer*. In one of the chapters, he explains how growth could be immensely dangerous (*and we thought growth is always good!*). Here are a few lines from the book which you can correlate with the context under consideration:

> *"Cancer is a disease caused by an uncontrollable growth of a single cell. In a normal cell, powerful genetic circuits regulate cell division and cell death. That this seemingly simple mechanism—cell growth without barriers—can lie at the heart of this grotesque and multi-faceted illness, is a testament to the unfathomable power of cell growth. Cell division allows us, as organisms: to grow, to adapt, to recover, to repair—to live. And, when distorted and unleashed, it allows cancer cells to grow—to live at the cost of our living."*

The sense that these lines carry heightens for us, when we discern the analogy between the phenomenon of uncontrolled cell growth, and uncontrolled ambition which drives us to live our life the way we do...every single day.

So have your pick of choice: whether to live life in a controlled fashion, or in an uncontrolled manner—just like the emperor of all maladies.

The second human quality that we would discuss in this chapter is our ***confidence***.

Just like the speed of our car, if our confidence is controlled, it can truly work wonders. But once we cross the defined 'city speed limits,' and add 'over' to the word confidence, we assure ourselves of failure—having embraced 'overconfidence.'

My observations leads me to the following conclusions…

> *Overconfidence leads to arrogance. Arrogance leads to bad attitude. Bad attitude breeds carelessness. Carelessness entices us to take wrong decisions. Wrong decisions will always deliver bad results.*

In the book, *Siddhartha*, by Hermann Hesse, which deals with the spiritual journey of an Indian, Siddhartha—during the time of The Buddha—there comes a situation when Siddhartha argues with Gotama over the philosophy of his teachings, and begs to differ with him. Gotama smiles at him and says, "Siddhartha, you are wise. You know how to talk wisely. But be aware of too much wisdom."

So as with the speed of driving, we must develop the habit of checking our confidence levels periodically. It is not at all easy to put brakes on our confidence level, because sometimes the line between confidence and overconfidence is so thin that we hardly realize while crossing it. But that is an art which we need to learn, if we wish to excel in the countless 'tests' that we face in life.

Even the laws of automobile engineering support this theory! The automobile companies educate us, stating that the wear and tear of the vehicle (*like our body*) is least when we drive it at normal speed, and in the run, we get the maximum fuel efficiency too (*similar to optimum utilization of our body's natural resources*). Under such circumstances, the car would need lesser maintenance (*similar to having complete peace of mind and lesser trips to the doctor*). With it, the life of the vehicle increases (*meaning: you live longer when you live free from stress*) dramatically.

I remember what **Milton Friedman** once said:

> **"We don't have a desperate need to grow. We have a desperate desire to grow."**

So next time when you go on a drive, remember: *safe driving is happy driving*. And do not forget the two essential qualities for your driving to be skilful. If you can drive safely, you know you can steer your ambitions, and your confidence too, to perfection.

49 Wanna Shine? Polish!

♣

There is a famous Indian movie producer-director who happens to be my favorite for years now. Being a huge fan of his, I have never ever missed a movie which came out of his production house. So having waited for months, I finally went to see his latest movie. But midway, I felt disappointed with his direction. Just because I am a die-hard fan of his I saw the entire movie, but did return with some bitterness. As expected, the movie *tanked* at the box office within the first week of its worldwide release.

After a few days, I happened to watch his interview on a famous television channel. The host predictably touched upon this very aspect of his latest movie: "What went wrong? Were *you* expecting different results? We never expected you to make such a disastrous movie. Your fans are angry all over the world."

He confessed, "You know what? After a few highly successful movies, I started spending all my time at the wrong places. I started facing more interviews, spent more time with the who's who of the film industry, undertook many new ventures as a producer and thus, drifted away from what I did best: directing movies. Little did I realize that I had parked my best skill—which had given me the fame and kept me in the limelight all these years—in the backyard. I had become overconfident. As a result, I assumed that the audience would accept anything and everything that I made. I lost my touch simply because I had given up practicing the skill that I was really good at. I clearly recall some of my friends warning me that I was making a crap of a movie. They had forewarned me about the consequences as well. But when you grow 'big' in life, you tend to get arrogant and careless. You hear, but you do not listen. And that is exactly what I did. I just ignored them and kept bathing in my own world of fame, limelight and showbiz. Now that the verdict is out, apart from losing millions of dollars, I have lost something more valuable... I have lost the confidence of my audience, which was earned through many years of pure blood and sweat.

With this latest movie, I have also learnt another hard fact of the show business: *you don't get a second chance*. Your audience always expects you to churn a blockbuster. It doesn't matter whether you are an actor or a director. They just want you to perform with equal dexterity, and at peak levels, all the time. This simply means that you have to be more careful than ever. One silly mistake, and you fall from such a height that you break all your bones in the process. The same financers, who had been pumping money into my ventures all these years—and had raked millions in profit—are now thinking twice, before continuing their association with me. All this is sad, but true. The most important lesson that I have learnt from my latest movie is: *if you want to keep shining, you have to polish your skills on a daily basis*. You can't allow dust to settle down on them, and you simply can't afford them to look outdated and old either. Sadly, I learnt it the hard way."

Having recorded the interview, I pondered over it and played it again. And as I did, I realized that I too had learnt a lesson that day from someone's life. I had also read about many C-level executives who suddenly drifted away after becoming hugely successful in their careers. They started: attending parties hosted by political honchos, distributing awards at fashion pageants and appearing on 'page 3.' They focused on getting more coverage in magazines like *Hello* and *O*, rather than *Fortune* and *Forbes*. The moment you see that happening to your favorite CEO, you know it is time to sell his company's stocks and move on to greener pastures. Recently, I saw stocks of a very large company, headed by a very charismatic person, going down by as much as 38%. The reason: he had been busy sponsoring sporting events, rather than concentrating on the real needs of his shareholders. All such people failed to realize that it was their performance, and nothing else, which had made them rich and famous.

Therefore, the rule is simple: the moment you stop practicing your skills and thus, stop honing them, you will be eaten away by a newborn competitor of yours. Some of the world's greatest business leaders have their *names* imprinted in history, *synonymous* with success—because they did not leave their 'true' skills till their last day in office. They were brilliant at distancing themselves from all the clutter that media brought, while it highlighted their fame and fortunes across numerous channels. They simply stayed away from the side-effects of fame, preferring to stay focused instead on that which brought them the fame!

The same 'rule' of life fits extremely well in the world of sports too. In fact, I have seen extremes in these cases. There are only a few dedicated sportspersons who have been churning gold medals for their country, year after year, while there are many who are 'one-time gold' wonders. You see them performing at their peak, and you start loving them. You even start worshipping some of them. But very soon, they are seen everywhere: in advertisements, in the electronic as well as the print media; as brand ambassadors, at charity events; and at 'page 3' parties, with all those arm candies dying for their attention. The only place you stop seeing them is the same old playground where, at one point in their life, they had sweated hard to earn all that they are now busy losing—to fame and stardom.

Well, I am not against brand endorsements at all. It indeed feels good to see your favorite sportsperson getting associated with the brands that you like, but not at the cost of their quality of play. They can't afford to lose their shine. They need to understand: the moment their performance drops, the same companies which had lined up at their doorsteps—with millions of dollars in cash for signing them up—would line up at their doorsteps again, but this time to cancel their contracts with them.

The message is loud and clear: never let the dust play spoilsport and diminish the lustrous charisma in you.

Peeping into the corporate world, I see this in practice more than anywhere else. Each year bright young kids join your company. Some of them work hard and impress you with their acumen. As a result, you reward them handsomely. But the very next year, you find them nowhere in the list of your star performers. Why did they disappear from the list? Because, people expect to be rewarded on a continual basis, but fail to realize that they too need to operate at their peak levels at all times for the same. And *even* when they are led to this reason, they do nothing about it. *They find it easier to swallow the reason, but it is hard for them to digest the reason that they themselves are the cause*. Ultimately, some of them get frustrated and shift to another company, while there is a dip in the performance levels of some as the fire in their belly loses intensity over time. And the ones who remain alive, are the ones who polish their skills, year-on-year, and surprise you with their consistent results—no matter what they work upon and what they get in return. When I look back to count such people who were good at polishing their skills, on a daily basis, the number that I am led to is even less than 10.

There is another interesting incident, worth sharing, in this context. A friend of mine follows his unique philosophy of changing jobs every two years. Ask him why, and he would respond with conviction: "I need variety and change. I work very hard in the first year to learn new things, and by the time I am into my second year the fire inside my belly goes off. So, I switch jobs to re-ignite the fire. It helps me perform at my peak levels." And I keep telling him (even though he is yet to listen), "It would be hundred times better if you re-ignite the passion and rediscover yourself, not by changing jobs but by polishing your skills at the same job. Nowadays, most of the companies are looking for that passion—but, along with stability. Till now, you have been able to survive with your philosophy. But very soon, you will not be marketable enough to land up with new jobs every couple of years."

Let us hope that he understands it sooner, rather than later.

I don't want him to meet me one day and declare, "You were right. But I learnt it the hard way."

50 The Hunter and the Cook Story

♦

This incident dates back to those years when I was entrusted with a pre-sales role for the very first time. Prior to that, I belonged to the coding world; and I enjoyed every bit of being in that tribe. But one day, my manager approached me and said, "I am shifting you to a new role, based on your personality and performance." Even though it meant parting ways, she was gracious enough to recommend my name for an elite team. My company was setting up this team for marketing new software packages to ward off stiff competition. I simply cannot describe all that went through my mind when I came to know of this decision. For me it meant leaving something which I knew very well, for something which I knew nothing of. The fear of failure made its presence known. Yet, excitement too was at its premium. The opportunity to do something new beckoned invitingly. As always, I took life the way it was dished out to me and agreed to get into the groove of a new role.

To be candid, until then I did not even know what pre-sales meant. I mean, I knew what sales meant and what marketing meant. But pre-sales? Never heard of it, man!

Very soon, I was transferred to a different office, right in the middle of the city and bubbling with action all the time. In my earlier role, I had become used to the quiet world around my cubicle, which sprung to life only for two reasons: when one of the fellow 'coders' from our tribe got stuck somewhere within the complex web of system designs, and for coffee breaks. But this new office, I tell you, belonged to a different tribe. The phone never stopped ringing, and no one would pick it up either! At times, I felt that my new tribesmen got their creative ideas only when the environment was extremely chaotic—and hence, it could be the reason why no one would ever pick up the ringing phone.

In my previous domain, I was a hero. People knew me by the name: Young Warrior. But here, it seemed everyone was a zero. No one knew anyone. No, 'hi'...no 'hello'...nothing. Greetings were absent, even when we had a direct eye contact with one another. Therefore, forget smiling at strangers. Initially, I felt completely disconnected from my surroundings. On the other hand, my old tribesmen were missing me and wanted me to come back. I too wanted to return...but that didn't happen and in retrospect, I am glad for the same.

Sometimes the steps that we take in life unleash circumstances which wash away the trail of the path traversed, carrying us forward on this journey of life. Thus, retracing the path and starting all over again, becomes very difficult. I had picked up my battle by then, and I was left with no choice but to fight it out.

Days went by and I started *liking* the chaos. I made new friends and began to settle down. One day, my new boss called the entire team for a meeting and announced, "You folks will be having a 2-day residential workshop, starting Monday. It will be conducted by a world-renowned sales enablement guru. He is coming to India just for you folks. So, make the best use of it while he is here. After this workshop you will be on your own to fight and survive." The meeting ended within 5 minutes (quicker than I could have ever imagined).

We shall refer to this guru as Mr. Z to honor his privacy.

The next Monday, we gathered in a packed conference room of a hotel, and awaited the arrival of our facilitator. After reading his brief profile, which was circulated amongst all of us in the morning, I found that his credentials were indeed impressive in the international arena as our boss had told. This further increased my excitement...and just then he arrived!

After the round of introductions, he started, "Kids, we will have a lot of time at our disposal to go through the material, which my assistant has already circulated to all of you. After all, the whole night is ours (he smiled, blinking both of his eyes). But before that, I want all of you to listen to the "Hunter and the Cook" story. Have you heard it before?" We all nodded in the negative. Thus he began and continued...for long...

The same is reproduced, in his own words...

> *"So kids, the story that I am going to tell you goes long back in history... when we used to live in caves, in closed communities. During that time, we used to have only two kinds of tribes within each community: the hunters and the cooks.*
>
> *The hunters would go out in the forest at dawn and would hunt for the whole day. By dusk, they would bring the killings back to the community. The cooks would then take over, and prepare food—out of those killings—for the entire community.*
>
> *Now, for a moment, consider the hunters who bring the killings back to their community, as the executives who bring revenue to the company...and the cooks who prepare food out of those killings, as the service delivery personnel. Both are important for a community as they cannot survive without one other. Yet, history tells us that the best-prized people were always the 'hunters' and not the 'cooks.' The hunters were always more valued by the community, compared to the cooks. To some, it may sound like the chicken versus egg story. But the truth is, history has always relied on hunters.*
>
> *From now on, I want all of you to be razor-sharp focused hunters. Most of you belonged to the 'cook' category before coming here, but not anymore! You will now have to leave those sweet memories behind, and get into the skin of a 'hunter.' Let there be others, who are happy and content being a 'cook.' You must start going to the fields, and make a killing for yourself and for your community. And believe me, you will be truly rewarded for what you bring back home. There are plenty of animals out there, waiting to be hunted. Make a killing, give it to a cook and move on. That is where your true value lies, and this should be your only motive in life from now on.*
>
> *However, there are few rules in the hunting game that you must always remember.*

Rule 1: *There will be plenty of animals, waiting to be hunted. A hunter has to do his homework well and kill the right-sized animal—the one that can satiate many empty stomachs at one go. Study the hunting fields where you would normally operate. Find out the areas that will work in your favor, and areas that can put you in danger. There will be days when you return empty-handed, and that is okay. You can't make a killing everyday. But the day you don't make a killing, you must spend the night empty stomach. Do not borrow and eat. That hunger, in turn, should drive you to become a better hunter when you go into the jungle the next day. Likewise, in the corporate jungle, focus on the right accounts and spend your time in areas which generate long-term revenue for the company. Just like a hunter has limited hours during the day—to make a killing—you too will have limited time to make a sale.*

Rule 2: *When you are out to kill a large animal, you will need to work in a group to make that killing. The hunter will have to work collaboratively with other talented hunters to make such a killing. He just can't rely only on his own skills to make such a large killing. If he does so, chances are, the animal might as well succeed in killing him. Therefore, in such cases, his 'teaming' skills will be of utmost importance. While one hunter may be good at shooting, another may be good at distracting the animal...while the third may be deft at trapping it using the bait. Leverage skills, to make a kill. Team-up with the right set of people to make that large kill. You don't have to be good in all the hunting areas. For that you have your fellow hunters, whose strengths must be leveraged to make that prized killing. Be a master of relations. Lastly, when you make such a killing, do not forget to thank all your fellow-mates who helped you with the killing. Let the community know that it was a joint effort. Do not try and become a hero when you know deep within, what actually killed that animal. Always remember that life is a continuous journey; you will need them again, whenever you encounter such a large animal in future.*

Rule 3: *A Chinese proverb says, "A hunter is as good as his spear." Always remember that. You are as good as the weapons that you use for hunting. So whenever you get time, sharpen your weapons. If you fail to do so, you will lose. In the corporate world, these weapons could be: your inter-personal skills, your presentation skills (i.e., the way you make and present proposals), the way you create those awesome looking proof-of-concept, etc. During those bad days, when you fail to make a killing, try* *and have a second look at the sharpness of your weapons. Most of the time, you would find that your weapons have become blunt and need another round of sharpening, before they can help you in making a kill again. Now, how do you sharpen those weapons? You have two ways to do it. You would either need a grinding stone or a forge and a foundry. The grinding stones in the corporate world are none other but your trusted advisors, mentors and true friends. Take their help when the time is rough and they will help you sharpen the weapon. The forge and the foundry, on the other hand, would be your trainers and the training facilities. This is the place where you can meet various skilled trainers, who would show—and teach you—innumerable ways to make a killing.*

Rule 4: *The community does not have a heart of its own. It is ruthless. If you don't make a killing for days, expect a changeover. The community would change your role and cast you away. A cook also faces the same danger. If you don't cook well, chances are, you would be moved out of that role. Neither a hunter nor a cook has the luxury of sitting on his laurels for long. If a hunter has killed a big animal, he remains a hero only till the kill is fully consumed by the community. As soon as the kill is eaten up, the community starts expecting the same level of heroism from him yet again. Similarly, a cook is respected and praised for the dinner he prepares for the community every day. And again, he too is remembered for preparing delicious food only till the food lasts. Once the food gets eaten up, the community quickly forgets the same, and expects delicious food the very next night. Bottom line is plain and simple: each day, in the life of a hunter and a cook, has to be a new day. The moment he becomes lazy or casual in his approach, he will be dethroned. So remember, whatever you do, you must do it well, with complete focus and dexterity. Otherwise, be ready to be overthrown by the next kid on-the-block.*

So, from today, become the best hunters and make your community proud of you. Go out and hunt! The whole jungle is yours to feast upon."

It goes without saying that the workshop was a huge success. I personally benefited immensely from it, and I am sure there must have been many who would affirm the same. Furthermore, I realized later that I had picked up the habit of putting the word 'tribe'—around everything—due to him and the story he told that day!

51 The '007' Principles

♥

Very early in my career, a time came when I was being transferred to a new project. But I had no any idea of the 'to be' technology that these people wanted me to work on. I was still very naïve, being barely few months old in the IT industry. I felt that a sudden change—that too, so soon—from what I was doing, was totally uncalled for. Hence, I requested my team leader to keep me with him and he nodded in a gentleman's 'yes.' It was only later that I found he himself had been transferred to this new project. ☺.

This project was for a very prominent American customer. The project was big enough for the customer to relocate its program manager to India, so that the entire program could be managed much more effectively. We came to know that he was an American citizen, in his mid-fifties. The kick-off date for the project was finalized and the project took off with a bang (read: party). The next day was going to be the first day of the project, and the team—comprising of 150 people—got an invitation for the formal kick-off. The meeting hall in the basement was crowded, bustling with all sorts of discussions flying around.

Soon, the program manager entered and greeted all of us. Within few minutes he explained: what his company did in the States; how they operated; what were his expectations from this project; and what was at stake. Then he switched over to sharing some of his experiences and working principles. And his speech—over the next 60 minutes—changed my life. While he was brilliant with his use of the English language, he was even better at holding the attention of the audience, by cracking timely jokes. The meeting, besides being informative and educative, thus had an added flavor: he made the environment lively and informal, and that served as the icing on a cake.

All that he shared was so enlightening that it is a pleasure to reproduce—even if a part of it—here.

And that too, in his own words...

"Those who know me well, often call me Bond, James Bond! (And he immediately made a gun out of his first two fingers, while folding the rest, and posed in a typical James Bond style. Predictably, we clapped hard like kids.) *Not because I have been appointed by 'M' for Her Majesty's secret service, but by my very own seven working principles. I call them "The '007' principles," which I have always followed, throughout my life. Let me tell you, they have not been lifted out of some magical fantasy, like the Lewis's Narnia's, but are very simple. Have you ever realized that we often tend to neglect life's simple rules and remember the ones that do not carry any value? I remember from my younger days that I used to make lot of mistakes in physics, and when my teacher used to show me the correct way of solving problems, I often realized that the root cause of the mistakes lay in my lack of understanding of the fundamental rules of physics.*

So now we begin...with **principle number 001**. *The first rule of the game is to understand that there is no—I repeat, no—substitute of hard work. I often see kids of your age running on the wrong path, thinking: short-cuts can take them closer to fame and money quicker than any other route. In doing so, they often neglect the main ingredient of the recipe for 'success'—which is nothing but hard work.*

Just like you can't substitute cheese while making pizza, you can't substitute hard work while 'making success.' Without cheese, you may still be able to make something quickly which could satisfy your hunger, but you cannot call it a pizza. Similarly, you may sometimes make quick money without working hard for it, and may satisfy your hunger to earn more. But you cannot call it success. I have seen people staking their hard earned money in lotteries, gambling and stock markets, in a bid to earn higher dividends—and quicker, at that—than what life has to offer. Do they win all the time? No. You cannot be lucky all the time.

So guys, as you get into this project, work hard. Working hard is directly under your control. No one messes with it. The harder you work, the more you will get that satisfying, rich feeling of having truly earned your stripes by following the right path: the path of hard work.

On the same topic of hard work, I have a small (real life) story to share. The day after graduating from one of the premier institutes, a son joined his father's business. On the first day, dressed like a thorough gentleman, he went to his father's cabin and asked with all the passion in the world, 'Dad, which department do I have to take over?'

His dad looked up and called someone over the phone. After a couple of minutes, an elderly guy entered the cabin and wished them. His father said, 'Son, from today, you will work under the guidance of Eddie, our mail room person for the past 30 years, and help him in his work.'

On hearing this, the son got the worst shock of his life. He had expected a cushy position, with all the great things around. However, without saying a word, he went away and started working. Days went by...and after ninety days, his dad called him in his cabin again. This time, the cabin was full of top executives from the company. He said, 'Looking at the way you have worked for the past three months, the board of directors have decided to promote you as the Chief Operating Officer (COO) of the company. Congratulations!'

With all the applause around the son was completely flabbergasted, and asked, 'Dad, why now and why not three months before?' The father smiled, and said, 'Son, there were many reasons to it.

First and foremost, I wanted you to show respect to the lowest paid person in the company. I wanted you to appreciate the work that Eddie has been doing for us over the last 30 years. In the first month, Eddie told me that you were not sincere with your job. But, by the second month, you picked it up and by the third, you were a pro, thoroughly enjoying the work which was given to you by Eddie. I wanted you to understand the fact that all jobs are good, provided you do it sincerely and with great passion. Moreover, I wanted to see if my son can do a petty job like scanning mails. After all, if you can't scan mails and shipments correctly, how can you expect me to believe that you would be able to pilot this company well? And last but not the least, I wanted you to earn respect of the people in the lowest rung of our company. Almost always, we choose the top management of the company without taking the opinion of the masses. And worst, these top executives then take decisions on behalf of the masses that the company constitutes of, without putting themselves in the shoes of the mass even for once. I am now confident that as the COO whatever decisions you would take on behalf of the company, you would, taking everyone into consideration and thus, will cut across all sections of manpower working for us.'

The reason for telling this story is clear. If we do our jobs well, we will always be successful. And remember: each one of us counts. Consider yourself to be one of the syllable in a large symphony. The symphony will sound perfect only when all the syllables play in a particular order, in tandem. If we miss one of the syllable, we will never be able to achieve a perfect Yanni-composition.

This brings us to ***principle number 002.*** *As per this rule, you should be good at 'asking.' Let me elaborate upon this. Most of the time, I see people hesitating to ask—be it at a grocery store or in a classroom or client meetings or project meetings. Do you know why? We are just too conscious: of what people might think and say, if we ask. We tend to assume that if we ask too much, people might term us as the dumb guy who asks too many questions. My dear friends, your assumption is incorrect! Here is my response in this context: you may think of* *such people as dumb, but if you do not ask and instead, start assuming everything on your own, then you might end up being called 'dumber.' Now, pick your choice: 'dumb' or 'dumber?'*

I have found from my rich experiences that most of the times when we fail, we fail having made the wrong assumptions. And why did we make the wrong assumptions? Because, we did not ask the right questions! Most of the projects go wrong because we are masters at making assumptions, and have made it an obvious choice for ourselves to follow. So, while assessing a new project, we rely more on assumptions than the hard facts (data, which we never ask our clients to provide). The end results are: budget overruns; gaps in client's expectations—between the designed systems vis-à-vis what we built for them; and finally, failure.

Similarly, on the personal front, I have come across many couples who fought over trivial issues. And when I went deep into what created all those confusions, the culprit that always emerged, was our very own 'Mr. Assumption.' Neither the wife nor the husband, took the pain of asking the truth from their partner. Instead, they just went ahead and 'assumed.' Having assumed, they started treating it like a fact, and then...you can very well imagine what the rest of the story would look like.

Do you know, how I overcame this habit of assuming? Let me tell you a little secret: if you remove 'ume' from 'assume,' it leaves us with 'ass!' (The hall filled with laughter.) Whenever I used to assume, I used to ask myself: 'Am I getting close to being called an ass later?' This mere thought always made me gather courage, to stand up and ask the right questions—rather than assume. So next time, when you get into such a situation, stand up and ask, and avoid being labeled an 'ass' in real life.

My ***principle number 003*** *revolves around respecting the governance models. How many times on Mother Earth you have heard about companies adopting 'open door' policies and encouraging flat organizational structures? I am sure, the answer would be: 'Countless.' And then there are some, who would even keep their cabin doors open—all the time—to prove how much aligned they* *are with this policy! But the truth that lies out there is, we do have structures and we do have governance models that need to be respected. Don't get carried away by the lucrative jargons that our HR uses all the time. I hope we don't have anyone from HR amongst us, otherwise I will be a dead fish, sooner than expected. (The crowd chuckled again.)*

All this would mean: you need to respect your boss all the time. The one who does your appraisal has to be respected. This holds true, in all corners of the world and for all the types of organizations. Being respectful, and being a sycophant, are two different things. All I am saying is, you need to be respectful—and at the same time, do not end up being a sycophant.

We have heard about 'skip level' meetings. But they make sense only when you have approached your immediate boss and have failed to get a reasonable solution to your problem. When such a thing happens, be honest with 'your boss' and take 'his okay' to approach 'his boss.' This builds trust—and nurtures openness—between you and your boss. Always remember what I term: 'access mechanism.' While you may have one-time access to your boss's boss, due to the so-called 'open door' policy or 'skip level' meetings, your boss has unlimited access to his boss. So, now you know what I mean? If you don't build trust with your boss, he will get unlimited chances of defending himself in front of his boss—and unlimited chances to portray you in the manner he wants to.

Here is another thing that I have observed many times. The young kids do not want to treat their boss as boss, simply because they feel that they have larger quantity of grey matter than their bosses. At times, it may be true, but remember the access mechanism I spoke about. So don't make that mistake—ever—in your career. Make your boss your best friend, and let him take care of your career. The governance models are at home too. I am sure your parents must have set some kind of rules for the rest of the family to follow. They may be unsaid, at times. But they don't harm you, as much as they do in the corporate life—if you choose to neglect them.

(He paused for a while and then continued.)

Now let me ask a question: have you ever met anyone who has been very passionate about the work that he/she has been doing? (The crowd nodded.) *Now tell me honestly, don't you feel good when you meet such people? Don't you feel passionate when you are in company of such people?* (The crowd nodded again.) *This brings me to my* ***principle number 004****. Practice passion in your life—in whatever you do—and inject it in people around you as well. The moment you inject it in others, you create a world-class high performance team for yourself. Such a team can do wonders for you and your company. Always remember that battles are won, not by strength, but by sheer power of passion—the passion to win at all costs, come what may. History is replete with 'happenings' when one kingdom lost the battle to the other simply because one of the kings was more passionate than the other and thus, could inject more fire in his army to kill and win. If your team is passionate, it can complete the tasks in lesser time than you can even think of.*

Read about the lives of all the great people that come to your mind: Gandhi, Jack Welch, Benjamin Franklin, Einstein, Lincoln...the list is endless. There is only one thing common to all of them: passion. Whatever they did, they did with great passion. So guys, be passionate about what you do. Trust me, you will be happy when you practice it regularly. Passion alone can distinguish you from others, and position you on a higher platform than your competitor(s).

So, what next? Hmmm...

*Next principle...****005****...is all about: being transparent, truthful and honest in your life. Of all my principles, this is the toughest to practice, while easiest to follow! I will tell you an easy way to handle this one. One of the biggest teachers that one can find in this context, are the typical kindergarten kids. They are innocent, very transparent and honest in accepting their mistakes. They don't know how to articulate lies. Learn from them. When we grow up, we get infected by a number of bad habits, present in the atmosphere around us.*

And we start telling lies, we become dishonest...and worse, we start believing that it is the only way to survive.

We start worrying about what others may feel and how the society would react. As a result, we fall into that hazardous trap that is created by the belief: 'heavens will not fall if I do this just once.' And then we commit our first mistake; the first mistake gives rise to the second and second to the third...and before we realize, it becomes a habit. We start telling lies as if it were a piece of cake. We not only become proficient in telling lies, we 'make' it 'natural.' We become dishonest because we want to get things quickly, rather than toiling hard to get them. Even worse, we carry these habits back home and start 'benefiting' from them, by implementing them in our personal relationships too. Picture this: you get late for dinner at your home and when your kids ask the reason, you are quick enough to use one of your habits to 'save' yourself. Your children and your spouse start bearing the brunt of these habits—day in and day out. And then, there comes a day, when they pick it up themselves and start applying them—back on you. The world is round and small, my dear! What you throw, comes back to you with a stronger force—even stronger than the one you used while throwing it. So, be honest, transparent and truthful in whatever you do. And rest assured, it will pay you handsomely in the long run.

I know I have taken quite a bit of time; but hey, hang on…it isn't lunch time yet. So bear with me for some more time. (The crowd cheers and urges him to continue.)

For ***principal number 006****, I have something to say about the mistakes we commit every day. First, tell your mind and your heart that it is okay to commit mistakes. While working on your projects, if you are not making mistakes, then something is surely not working out well! I see it as an indication of gaps in your learning. Unless you make mistakes, you can't learn and move up the value chain. So, never get upset when you commit them. Making mistakes is not bad. It becomes bad only when you commit them repeatedly. That, to me, shows a lot about your attitude towards life, which is nothing but 'careless.' And I simply hate careless folks. While they will ruin themselves for sure, they will* *infect others too. Most of the time, when our fixed-price projects fail, they do so for two reasons:*

- *We fail to estimate it correctly, by not asking the right questions—relying more on assumptions instead.*
- *The team's composition: many careless folks, who never learnt from their mistakes.*

Another aspect with respect to committing mistakes, which is true for the younger folks like you, is that, even after committing mistakes, I have seen some of them not even accepting the fact that they had committed one. To me, this is even more serious than committing one. You can correct a person, if he acknowledges that he made a mistake. But you can't correct someone who does not even realize that he just made one. Instead of accepting that they did wrong, the younger kids are quick to put the blame on someone else and walk away nicely. Remember the long hands of the law, which none can escape? No matter how fast you run or how long you run, you will ultimately be caught one day. So, use your mistakes to improve yourself. All the great people—you could think of—committed lot of mistakes. But it was their ability to accept them, and learn from them, which set them apart. If you 'read' Gandhi, you will come to know about the countless mistakes he committed in his youth. But what made him one of the greatest men ever on this earth, was his unique ability to learn from them and his subsequent pledge, to which he diligently adhered: not to repeat them in future.

And finally...here I am...with the last principle in my list: ***the 007 principle****. This one, if implemented properly, can put you in a different league altogether. But, if neglected, it could become the single most important reason for your failure too. It pertains to our ability to react positively to any feedback which is passed to us (in any form).*

In my entire career, I have come across many C-level and top executives who had been brilliant in their respective professions. Yet, I saw them failing miserably when it came to accepting feedback gracefully. That is the reason why you have only one Jack Welch and only one Lee Iacocca on this planet. As far as the rest of the herd is concerned, I label them as 'business as usual' guys.

There might be instances when you feel that the feedback being passed along is not correct—and that feeling is perfectly fine as per my perception. But, while it is important to judge the quality of feedback being passed, more important it is for you to fine-tune your brain to accept it. When I was young and my parents used to pass their feedback to me—on various aspects of mine—I used to revolt, yelling, 'It is my life; so let me deal with it.' But after so many years now, I realize that while I dealt with my life on my own terms, the journey was far more painful—compared to what I would have experienced, had I listened to them and undertaken the journey as they had suggested.

See, facts are facts! Feedback is just a way of stating those facts to you. It is completely your choice: whether you want to accept the facts by listening to others, or let your life force you to accept them—sooner, than later. You cannot change these facts. However, by ignoring them, you are cooking up disaster. The same facts would catch you, when you are fully unaware of them—as in the game of hide and seek. You simply cannot hide for the rest of your life. The game has to end and you have to get caught. That is how the game is played, and that is how your life is played out too. So next time someone gives you a feedback, do not turn a deaf ear. Open your ears wide, and listen. They will make your journey far easier than you could ever imagine.

I know all this sounds like heavy-duty stuff. And probably, you all are too young to understand all of this at one go. But, the sooner you get its essence, the better you will become—to survive and thrive in this world.

Just follow this simple rule: all the skyscrapers that you see every day—while coming to your office—stand tall because they are built on solid foundations. The principles that we set in our life, for ourselves, determine how tall our careers would grow and how stable and deep-rooted our relationships would be. So choose them wisely, because they become your destiny.

Thank you all and God bless!

Over to the lunch table now, and be ready for your first day at the project tomorrow. I must tell you, upfront, that it is going to be hell of a roller coaster ride for everyone. ☺."

Whenever I ponder over these simple, yet timeless principles, I notice that we hardly get to meet such people in our life who would take the pain to tell us what worked well for them and what did not. I don't know how many of us (present on that day) follow his principles till date. But I know for sure, that whosoever followed (and follows) them, must be having a ball with their life. ☺.

52 Say Cheese!

♠

As is the first chapter of a book special, so is the last. So as we come to the last—the fifty second card, in this pack that this book is for me—it is just the 'right' one for the purpose, and I hope my readers too would agree with me!

I still remember those days, when every year our school photographer used to set us up, in step-wise fashion according to our heights—along with our class teacher—and just before taking the shot, would shout, "Say cheese!" And all of us would repeat aloud, without even giving it a second thought. It took me many years to realize how important these two words are and how they bless us with one of the priceless things: smile, that alights our face.

I am sure, none is untouched by the aura of smile. Smile is a grace that brings happiness to the lives of all who are touched by it. It was for the same reason that I had reserved the discussion on the same—*for, in and as*—the last chapter. From the very beginning, I wanted to end my book by sharing insights on how we can bring smiles in everybody's life through small and simple acts of love. As Frank Crane brilliantly observed, "It takes so little to make people happy. Just a touch, if we know how to give it, just a word fitly spoken, a slight readjustment of some bolt or pin or bearing in the delicate machinery of a soul."

Smile is such a powerful force that it can really work

wonders—and does too. Delhi is well-known for its rudeness on the roads. Many a times, there would be rash drivers, trying to overtake you from the wrong side, honking incessantly. If you are even a minute late in giving them the pass, they would soon overtake and show you the middle finger, for sure. Whenever it has happened with me, the only trick I play is, look at them, waive hand and give a big smile. Want to know, what I get in return?

Well, sometimes, it is a surprised face (surprised, because they do not expect peace on Delhi roads and calmness from Delhites). At other times, they look at me as if I have gone crazy. But yes, there have been occasions when I have also seen their frustration change into a broad smile, as they reciprocate happily.

Smiles are infectious. They infect everyone and anyone who comes within the perimeter of the person infected with smile! And the after-effects remain for long, even after the infected person has moved away from his original coordinates. However, with the kind of lives that we all live, we have vaccinated ourselves against this infection—thus living a life, immune to smiles.

I remember one of my best friends telling me once...

"You must never dissociate yourself from people who are cheerful, irrespective of whether they have a social status comparable to yours or not. Cheerful people are turning into a rare species with each passing day. Life has become so fast-paced—and challenging—that it has killed the cheerful child which once resided in all of us. Most of the time, we sulk at not having enough money to spend. On the other hand, if we do have enough to spend, then we sulk because we do not have the time to spend it. But you know what? Happiness comes free of cost, and is available 24×7. All you have to do is, know the art of allowing it to come out in the most expressive manner. And once you master the art of keeping yourself happy, all the time, the world will be at your feet. People would then love to get associated with you, and that is quite natural. If you think a little deeper you will realize: *no one wants to get associated with people who always discuss problems and issues.* You already have a bagful of them on your side, right? On a similar note, your best friends are those who make you feel happy from within—those, who bring a smile on your face whenever they meet. Hence, you *must* choose one such friend as your life partner. After all, if your best friend can make you happy—even when you meet only for a while—she/he can make you happy for the rest of your life too."

I took his advice very seriously and married my best friend.☺.

A profound insight in this context was shared by a person I used to work for. He was a proponent of spreading happiness in the lives of others. He used to tell me, "Have you ever wondered: if a smile of 5 seconds can bring life to a photo being clicked, what it would bring to your life, if you keep smiling through the thick and thin of your life?"

There is another very good friend of mine, who recently shared his unique habit: "I have this weird habit of capturing all the moments on a camera. I always carry a mobile phone which has a great camera. I love to capture moments; not just the special ones, but also the ordinary ones. It is up to us to treat our ordinary moments as 'ordinary,' or as 'special' as they could be. People celebrate special days like birthdays, anniversaries, etc. But to me, each day that we spend with love, is a day to celebrate. Therefore, every day is a special day for me and since it is special, it calls to be captured."

He suddenly became nostalgic and continued, "There was a time, when nothing worked well between me and my wife. Misunderstandings, communication gaps…you know how it goes. In fact, a time comes when such things happen with almost every couple. But, in our case it stretched beyond the 'normal level' and thus, we started drifting apart. Distances, which looked small at the beginning, suddenly enlarged and took nasty turns. Deep within, we both knew that we loved each other; yet it was just not working out well. Then came our marriage anniversary. She was putting up with her best friend. I decided to give our relationship one last try, and made a large collage out of all the pictures that I had taken during our good old days. Those campfires, dancing at the party, celebrating our 'first date anniversary,' watching movies together, and walking for miles...hand-in-hand...along the seashore. I went to her friend's place, gifted it and came back. Next morning, when the doorbell rang and I opened the door, I could not believe my eyes... She was standing right in front of me, with the collage in one hand and her purse in the other. She threw everything and hugged me. That very day I thanked God for blessing me with this habit which saved my marriage from falling apart".

I am reminded of another person, who was gifted with this unique gift that is being discussed in this chapter. He used to work for me. During all those years that we worked together, I hardly saw him working under stress or any kind of tension. It was not that his life was not hell at work (that kind of life does not exist in my kind of setup); but the way he handled stress was his USP. Even during the most difficult periods of our 'red zone' projects, he would operate effectively and always gave me the status of the project with a smiling face. A smile, which exuded the confidence of success. A smile, which reflected the calmness of a peaceful mind. It was a smile of a person whose company would never let you feel low in life.

As a matter of fact, I always try and remember what **Henry Drummond** quoted:

> ***"You will find—as you look back upon your life—that the moments that stand out, the moments when you have really lived, are the moments when you have done things in the spirit of love."***

The crux lies in:

- Being happy with what we are and who we are.
- Understanding, that this life is too small to hold grudges against people.

Life is lived fully, only if we promise ourselves to live a life spreading the infection called 'smile!'

With this beautiful thought, I leave you all with all my best wishes, for living your life as blissfully as possible, and to be as thankful as possible, to Him, for allowing you to spend each day in good health and in the company of your family and friends. After all, everything else is secondary.

Till we meet again—and even after—keep spreading the infection please...

Say cheese!

Epilogue

♣

It won't end here...

Writing my first book has been a wholesome—and hence, satisfying—experience. I never realized that writing a book was so tough, until I wrote one! Now I understand—in retrospect—fully, the meaning of what my father-in-law taught me. It was one of the great lessons of life, which I received soon after my marriage. He said, "There are only two ways to learning in life. One, by listening to what others tell you; and two, by experiencing it yourself." *Prior to writing a book*, I always *used* to think of it as a child's play—imagination made manifest, of a person blessed with the luxury of free time. I was so damn wrong...and that I have learnt the hard way. ☺.

Here is another honest admission...

When I started working on this project, I assumed, a period of 20 weeks would be enough to complete this book. Well, I had thought: *it should not take longer, to write just about hundred pages*. Only when I had started writing, did I realize, I had underestimated the 'whole thing'—by as much as 50 additional weeks! No prior experience of writing a book, and my existing workload at office, made it very difficult for me to complete this book within the stipulated time.

At times, my mind poked me that maybe I had taken a wrong decision. I kept missing my personal deadlines one after the other, and felt like such a failure.

I remembered what Ray Kroc said, when one of the reporters commented, "Sir, you are very lucky. You became an overnight success." His repartee was, "Yes. That is true. But you do not know how long the night was!"

By the time I reached the last few chapters, I realized that the earlier chapters were in no way comparable to the ones I wrote later. I had always seen how artificial intelligence worked in reel life. But to see it in real life was altogether different and unique experience. I became more refined in bringing my thoughts to words and thus, set another deadline to rewrite some of the chapters that I had written earlier. This took an additional toll on me, and sapped my energy even further.

But whatever happens, happens *only and only* for the best. Time and again, God has graciously proved the same to me and thus, sustained my belief in the many "Life lessons" that God has taught me over the years. At different times, God has met me in different forms: family members, friends, colleagues, customers, teachers and mentors. And again, at times, as a complete stranger, passing on the priceless wisdom, that one should learn through and from the ups and downs in life.

I am also thankful for God's blessings that enabled me to understand the complex web of human relations in a lucid manner and thus, deal with them in profound ways. Each person and relation is unique, and needs a special kind of handling: a *customized handling*. Hence methods for the same are exclusive and unique to each relation. We, as humans, often make mistakes by assuming: one size would fit all and one approach would solve all our problems. Such an approach sounds like a true path to eternity. But in reality, it is our ability to treat every human being and every relationship exclusively which makes us a truly successful human being—a master of relationships we thus become.

Ever since I started writing, I have become a far better human being than what I used to be. My ability to think, and derive logical trees out of life's complex structures, has improved significantly. I have become quieter. I speak less now...instead, I have become a better listener. I can meditate better. I laugh aloud.

I help others more often. I derive happiness by making others happy. I always loved my family, and now, I love them even more. I miss my father and his gifted abilities, whenever I think of him.

My eyes see only the beautiful, no matter how difficult the situations are. My heart beats *only for love* and *not for hatred*. My mind is more focused than ever. My ego is a thing of the past. My prejudices are now buried deep below the ground of understanding. I have become better at saying, "Thanks" and "Sorry." I have become even better at acknowledging my strengths and weaknesses.

I have become a better driver—on roads as well as in life! I now understand the "Rabbit and the snail story" with further clarity. *I now understand that happiness lies in giving and not in taking.* I have become better at loving humans more, than money. I have become better at valuing time and accepting the fact that there are no 'time machines' in real life. I have understood the power of self-evaluation. I have realized how difficult it is to wear someone else's shoes, and why new shoes hurt. I have understood the power of emotions and how they could work in my favor. I have become better at kissing my failures and kicking my fears. I know now: *the most delicate thing in this world is not a Faberge egg, but the trust and belief that others put in you.* I have learnt how important it is to know our body and stay connected with our soul.

Bottom line is: I have started respecting and loving life more than ever. I am loving it, and living it one day at a time.

One thing that kept me going all these months is the undying love and patience of my wife; and I feel very happy and proud as this book reaches completion. *If nothing else, I could at least make her belief come true.*

My son still feels there will be no takers for this book, and I tell him, "You better start saving some dollars. At least that way, I will have two buyers: you and your mom! And if nothing works at all, here is plan B: I will buy a few copies, and donate it to your school library. Howzzat? " ☺.

As you read these last few lines—in this *pack of 52 cards*—I am glad to share an information with you: I have already started writing my second book. (My son will jump out of the window when he comes to know about this!) It would be a logical extension of the first one, i.e., this one. After all, life has so much to teach and offer every day, worth recording in the form of books and memoirs.

So, yes! I will be back...

ABOUT THE AUTHOR

The author works as an Associate Director for a leading US based multinational corporation. For the past few years, he has been dealing with "life" insurance based products and services on the professional side. An engineer by education, he believes that "life" is the greatest teacher of all times and one who understands life needs no further education to survive and be successful in this world.

However, on the personal side and for the last many years, he has been insuring and managing complex yet sweet "life" relations woven around his family, friends, colleagues, customers and well-wishers. Based in Delhi (India), he blissfully enjoys each day of his life with his wife and his 12-year old son.

He is closely associated to The Being Human Foundation, dedicated to the education and healthcare of the under-privileged kids and would continue to donate all the collections received from his books in the past and in the future. He believes that it is "his" way of giving it back to the society.

If anyone is interested in donating to the foundation (www.beinghumanonline.com), he can contact the author at sumeet.jain@gmail.com

Many Paths Many Answers

A Book On Corporate Spiritualism And Meaning Of Life

Dr. Hari Parameshwar

Become Incredible

More Powerful Than The Will To Win Is The Courage To Begin

Jordan Wirsz

The Cup of Life

A Journey Towards Self Contemplation

Seeta Rajesh Nawagekar